PRENTICE-HALL FOUNDATIONS OF PHILOSOPHY SERIES

Virgil Aldrich	PHILOSOPHY OF ART
William Alston	PHILOSOPHY OF LANGUAGE
Stephen Barker	PHILOSOPHY OF MATHEMATICS
Roderick Chisholm	THEORY OF KNOWLEDGE
William Dray	PHILOSOPHY OF HISTORY
Joel Feinberg	POLITICAL PHILOSOPHY
Wiliam Frankena	ETHICS
Martin Golding	PHILOSOPHY OF LAW
Carl Hempel	PHILOSOPHY OF NATURAL SCIENCE
John Hick	PHILOSOPHY OF RELIGION
John Lenz	PHILOSOPHY OF EDUCATION
Willard Quine	PHILOSOPHY OF LOGIC
Richard Rudner	PHILOSOPHY OF SOCIAL SCIENCE
Wesley Salmon	LOGIC
Jerome Shaffer	PHILOSOPHY OF MIND
Richard Taylor	METAPHYSICS

Elizabeth and Monroe Beardsley, editors

PHILOSOPHY

OF MIND

FOUNDATIONS OF PHILOSOPHY SERIES

Jerome A. Shaffer

University of Connecticut

PRENTICE-HALL, INC.   ENGLEWOOD CLIFFS, N. J.

PHILOSOPHY OF MIND, Shaffer

FOUNDATIONS OF PHILOSOPHY SERIES

Current printing (last number):
10 9 8 7 6 5 4 3 2 1

PRENTICE-HALL   INTERNATIONAL,   INC.   London

PRENTICE-HALL OF AUSTRALIA, PTY. LTD.   Sydney

PRENTICE-HALL   OF   CANADA,   LTD.   Toronto

PRENTICE-HALL OF INDIA PRIVATE LTD.   New Delhi

PRENTICE-HALL   OF   JAPAN,   INC.   Tokyo

To Olivia,

Diana, and David

FOUNDATIONS

OF PHILOSOPHY

Many of the problems of philosophy are of such broad relevance to human concerns, and so complex in their ramifications, that they are, in one form or another, perennially present. Though in the course of time they yield in part to philosophical inquiry, they may need to be rethought by each age in the light of its broader scientific knowledge and deepened ethical and religious experience. Better solutions are found by more refined and rigorous methods. Thus, one who approaches the study of philosophy in the hope of understanding the best of what it affords will look for both fundamental issues and contemporary achievements.

Written by a group of distinguished philosophers, the Foundations of Philosophy Series aims to exhibit some of the main problems in the various fields of philosophy as they stand at the present stage of philosophical history.

While certain fields are likely to be represented in most introductory courses in philosophy, college classes differ widely in emphasis, in method of instruction, and in rate of progress. Every instructor needs freedom to change his course as his own philosophical interests, the size and makeup of his classes, and the needs of his students vary from year to year. The sixteen volumes in the Foundations of Philosophy Series—each complete in itself, but complementing the others—offer a new flexibility to the instructor, who can create his own textbook by combining several volumes as he wishes, and can choose different combinations at different times. Those volumes that are not used in an introductory course will be found valuable, along with other texts or collections of readings, for the more specialized upper-level courses.

ELIZABETH BEARDSLEY MONROE BEARDSLEY

ACKNOWLEDGMENTS

This book is very much the product of twelve fruitful and happy years at Swarthmore College. Much of the material in it has been tested (and often found wanting) by the Swarthmore students, who taught me more than I ever taught them. I am much indebted to long discussions over the years with my Swarthmore colleagues, who have included Richard Brandt, Monroe Beardsley, Michael Scriven, Jaegwon Kim, Charles Raff, Hans Oberdiek, Richard Schuldenfrei, and neighboring Charles Dyke and Elizabeth Beardsley. To the editors of this series, I owe a special debt for their very helpful suggestions, unfailing tact, and remarkable ability to refrain from ever asking, despite countless opportunities, how the book was coming along. For secretarial help, I am grateful to Mrs. Mary Renneisen, Mrs. Dodie Halliwell, and, above all, Mrs. Edith Cohen. I now look to my new colleagues at the University of Connecticut to help me write a better book.

I wish to thank my parents, who brought me to consciousness, and my children, Diana and David, who gave me an object lesson in the miracle of consciousness. My wife, Olivia, has been a constant source of inspiration and confidence.

JEROME A. SHAFFER

CONTENTS

INTRODUCTION

1

The soul   When I was a boy, one of the burning issues of afterschool discussion was whether or not people have *souls*. Some argued that people must have souls, since they would not be different from animals if they did not. Others claimed that people are *not* different from the other animals so if people have souls, then the other animals, even the worms, have souls also. And how about death? If there were no soul, then death meant the end of *everything* for that person, a possibility too horrible to contemplate. Anyhow, what is the point of life if it ends with such absolute finality in death? But if people have souls, then what do these souls look like and where are they located? What little we knew about anatomy made it unlikely that any surgeon could, in operating on a person, discover his soul. So if people have souls, what are they? It was all too mystifying for us.

    Men have gone on being mystified by these and related issues for as long as we have records of human thought. We know that the ancient Greeks speculated about it at length twenty-five hundred years ago. And we know that many of the fundamental questions they raised are still unanswered today. They deal with some of the most obscure and impenetrable matters facing man as he attempts to understand himself, his world, and his place in it.

    It will be the task of this book to explore some of these questions and see what progress has been made in attempting to answer them.

1

What is the soul? The history of this concept is a long one. The ancient Hebrews, one of the earliest peoples to formulate such a concept, took the soul to be whatever it was in a body which made it *alive*, made it a living thing rather than a dead thing. They used the Hebrew word for "breath" to refer to the soul, presumably because it is such an important sign of *life*. This animating force was believed to reside in the blood.

The early Greeks added a new feature. For them, the soul was separable from the body, something that could continue to exist when the body died. Death, for the Hebrews, had been nothing but the end of life and of the animating force, the soul. For the Greeks, death was merely the *withdrawal* of the animating force from the body. Some of the Greeks, for example the Pythagoreans (famous for their mathematical discoveries), believed that the soul, after withdrawing from one body, would enter another; that is called transmigration. The Pythagoreans believed that any body capable of life could serve as the home of a soul, and they believed that the humble *bean* was an especially receptive home for the soul. It must be said that their *reasons* for so honoring the bean were not very compelling; namely, that a germinating bean sprout looks like a human fetus, and that crushed bean seeds left in the sun smell like human seed.

Although we have here, so far, the concept of a soul as separable from a body and capable of transmigrating from one body to another, we still have the notion that the natural place of a soul is in some *body*. It is in the writings of Plato that we can find the first explicit statement of the soul as something that can exist apart from any body whatsoever. In fact, for Plato, the ideal state of the soul is disembodied existence, in which the soul, having escaped the "prison" of the body, can live among the eternal and final Realities forever.

Aristotle, a student of Plato, provided the major alternative to the Platonic concept of the soul. He rejected the idea of the soul as an entity separable from the body and took the soul to be the structure and functioning of the body itself, or, as he put it, the "form" of the living human body. Since one cannot have the form without the body which has that form, the soul cannot exist disembodied.

The word "soul" does not have the wide currency it used to have, and this is true not only in everyday life but also in the technical fields of philosophy and psychology. There are a number of reasons for this. First, there has always been a temptation to take the word "soul" to refer to some sort of *physical* thing, a very ethereal gas, a shimmering sphere, a diamond-like nugget. To this day there are peoples who make sure a window is open near the body of a dying man to allow the soul to escape. But the existence of such a physical entity inside our body has been completely discredited as our scientific knowledge of human anatomy has developed. Second, the word has been closely associated with a particular set of theological beliefs, and especially with beliefs in an immortal soul which may dwell in a heavenly or hellish afterlife. It is almost a flat contradiction to speak of a *mortal* soul. Since such beliefs are no longer part of the common set of beliefs we all take for granted and do not question, we tend to avoid a word like "soul" which has certain theological associations. Finally, the term brings together two somewhat different ideas: that of a *living* thing in general and that of a *special kind* of living thing, a thinking and, perhaps, morally aware or spiritually sensitive thing. It has become increasingly important to distinguish these concepts, as we have come to see the great differences between the lower and higher orders of living things. For these reasons it is preferable to use a term that does not connote either the materiality or immortality of the soul, and allows us to distinguish intelligent creatures from the rest of living things. In the present day, the term most commonly used in place of "soul" is the word "mind." Hence the title of this book and of the field of thought it is about.

The mind   Just as it is tempting to think of the soul as a *physical thing*, so it is tempting to think of the mind as a *thing* of a non-physical kind. But so to conceive the mind is to adopt a particular philosophical theory about the mind, a very controversial one at that. We do not wish to begin this inquiry by assuming outright some particular, debatable view. We can use the term "mind" without thinking of the mind as an object, just as we can use the expression "time of day" without thinking of it as an object. But what are we to understand by this term?

Consider how the word "mind" is used in our language. We speak of changing one's mind, speaking one's mind, losing one's mind, being put in mind of something, having a mind to do something, having half-a-mind to do it, being of two minds about doing it. One can be strong-minded, tough-minded, weak-minded, or feeble-minded. One can be open-minded, sports-minded, single-minded, pure-minded, high-minded, simple-minded, or foul-minded. Can we ever hope to find some core meaning or common feature in this welter of expressions?

Progress can be made if we consider some of the ways "mind" is used as a verb:

Please mind the baby while I am out. *[look after, take care of]*
Mind the low ceiling. *[look out for, be careful of]*
Does he mind his parents? *[obey]*
Mind your own business. *[concentrate upon]*
Mind your manners. *[pay attention to]*
Did you mind when no one asked you to dance? *[care]*

Although all these uses differ somewhat, as the particular meanings given in the brackets indicate, they do seem to share a common feature, that of being conscious or aware of something, paying heed or attention, taking particular notice of something. It is this common feature, *consciousness*, which may be said to be a central element in the concept of *mind*.

If we were asked to give a general characterization of the branch of philosophy called philosophy of mind, we might say that it is that branch particularly concerned with the nature of consciousness, with what kinds of things are conscious or are capable of consciousness, and with all those phenomena (we will call them "mental phenomena") to which *only* beings capable of consciousness are subject. Relevant here are mental phenomena such as ways of being conscious (hearing, remembering, imaging, considering, expecting). Other mental phemonena are processes or states of what is conscious at the time; one must be conscious in order to feel happy, make a decision, deduce a conclusion, or inadvertently do something. Others are those states which presuppose not that the subject is actually conscious at the time, but merely that he has been conscious at some time; only of a being that has been conscious can we say that he is now in a coma or that he believes that all men are created equal or that he is stingy or that he wants to go to Europe.

We may put this in the most general terms by saying that the philosophy of mind is concerned with all mental phenomena, where "mental phenomena" is to be understood as all phenomena that exclusively involve beings capable of consciousness. (This characterization is not very illuminating, of course, since we must still clarify what "consciousness" is.)

The varieties of mental phenomena It would be useful if we could say that all mental phenomena fall into some manageable number of categories. It has been suggested, for example, that the mind has three basic capacities or "faculties" as they were called; namely, "cognition" (knowing), "affection" (feeling) and "volition" (willing); each mental phenomenon was supposed to be the result of the operation of these faculties. Thus under cognition, we would have sense perception, memory, introspection, intuition, inference and other sources of knowledge. Under affection we would have sensation, emotions, moods, personality traits, and other manifestations of feeling. Under volition, we would have motives, desires, deliberation, decisions and choices, strivings and tryings, and actions, all the factors influencing and exhibiting acts of will.

These faculties were postulated to *explain* the existence of the various mental phenomena. It was their hidden operations which were supposed to result in the production of sense perceptions, memories, and the rest. However, it has turned out that this postulation has no explanatory force whatsoever, since the only evidence we have for the existence of these faculties is the existence of the very mental phenomena they were intended to explain. They do not lead us to new mental phenomena, nor do they give us any better understanding of the already familiar mental phenomena. Thus the notion of basic faculties of the mind has been abandoned in modern thought.

As a *classification* of mental phenomena, this tripart division fares no better. There are all sorts of phenomena that do not fall happily into any of these classes. For example, to which faculty does *believing* belong? If we put it into the cognition bundle, where do we put its more affective brothers, having faith, trust, or confidence? Where do we put *feeling* confident or convinced or certain? How about disbelief, distrust, suspicion, or misgivings? Is it an exercise of cognition to have a hunch, foreboding, or presentiment? If I regret that something has happened, am I in a two-part state, with a belief that it has happened (cognition) plus a feeling of regret (affection)? But the parts are *not* separate and independent, as can be seen if we try to imagine the feeling of regret *without* the belief. Furthermore, if the alleged feeling of regret is accompanied not only by the belief that it has happened, but also by the belief that two plus two equals four, then do I regret also that two plus two equals four? And it will not help if we add that the feeling of regret must be caused by the belief, for when the teacher calls "Jones," my regret may be caused by my belief that my name is Jones, without my regretting that my name is Jones. Or again, is a *very strong feeling* that something will occur a case of a very strong affection or a very strong cognition? How about the *vague* feeling that something is wrong—a vague affection or a vague cognition? Examples of phenomena that defy this classification could easily fill the entire book.

Furthermore, we have lumped together under the same heading very different sorts of phenomena. For example, under cognition would go our knowledge of our present surroundings through sense perception, our knowledge of the past through memory, our knowledge of the future through inference, our knowledge of our present states of mind through introspection, and our knowledge of our own future actions through decision. But it is very misleading to put these together as one kind of phenomenon. For since we have various organs for sense perception, we might look (in vain) for an organ of memory. Since, in memory, we know our own past, we might puzzle about how we can know the future when it is still to happen. Since we know the future only on the basis of evidence, we might wonder what our evidence is by which we know our own present states of mind. And since we know our own decisions by introspection, we might construe our knowing what we shall do, once we have decided what to do, as either making an inference from the decision to the future or, worse yet, introspecting the future. Similar muddles will occur if we treat the phenomena under the headings of affection or volition as of the same basic nature.

The fact of the matter is that neither the tripart division of cognition, affection, and volition, nor, it would be safe to say, any simple division can do justice to what goes under the heading "philosophy of mind." This is not to say that no classification of mental phenomena will prove useful; however, the present mood in the philosophy of mind is to avoid any rigid classifications. The most important recent contributions to this subject have consisted in bringing out the important *differences* between phenomena that hitherto have been taken to be phenomena of the same sort. To take one example, pleasure and pain have often been taken to be opposite ends of a single dimension of sensation, distinguished only by degree. Thus, in moral philosophy, utilitarians like Bentham believed that one could arithmetically combine the positive quantities (pleasure) and the negative quantities (pain) to determine the sum total of pleasure-pain that a particular act would produce, and thereby evaluate it. But contemporary philosophers, led by Gilbert Ryle,[1] have pointed out that whereas the word "pain" is the name of a bodily sensation, "pleasure," typically, is not the name of a sensation at all. If someone is in pain as a result of rowing, it makes sense to ask *where* in his body he feels the pain. But if someone gets

[1] *The Concept of Mind* (New York: Barnes and Noble, 1949; Penguin paperback, 1963), Chapter IV, sec. 6; see also Ryle's contribution to the symposium "Pleasure" in *Proceedings of the Aristotelian Society*, Supplementary Vol. 28 (1954).

pleasure from rowing, it does not make sense to ask *where* he feels the pleasure. Here "pleasure" means "enjoyment," and its opposite is "displeasure," not "pain." This is why masochism does not involve inconsistency, although it does involve abnormality. A man who finds pain pleasurable finds pain enjoyable; it is not that he finds pain to be the opposite of painful.

Mental phenomena can be thought of as a large network of roads that crisscross, overlap, parallel each other at places and diverge at others. In such a network, there will be regions in which large numbers of roads converge in a cluster. So we can think of the hallowed trinity of cognition, affection, and volition as convergences of large numbers of mental phenomena. In the neighborhood of cognition we will find thought and belief, understanding, imagining, paying attention and noticing, perceiving, remembering and other cases of knowing, and so on. The vicinity of affection includes bodily sensations, feelings, emotions, moods, and frames of mind. And volition is in the region of desires, motives, decisions, intentions, trying, acting, pretending, and traits of behavior. (These more detailed phenomena should themselves be thought of as networks rather than individual roads.) Although it is far beyond the scope of this book to examine all these phenomena, as one would in a complete study of the philosophy of mind, we will consider a number of these concepts and, in particular, devote Chapter 5 to some problems concerning intentions, actions, and related concepts.

The relation of philosophy of mind to other disciplines The network analogy applies not only to the subdivisions of mental phenomena but to the very field of philosophy of mind itself as it is related to other fields of inquiry. The philosophy of mind crisscrosses at many points with other areas of philosophy.

For example, insofar as the philosophy of art deals with aesthetic *experiences*, ethics with moral *feelings*, the theory of knowledge with sense *experience*, the philosophy of law with *motives and intentions*, and the philosophy of religion with mystical *experience*, they all overlap the philosophy of mind. And there are many other places where these fields intersect. But it is perhaps with metaphysics that the philosophy of mind most often overlaps, for the latter's most basic questions concern the status and nature of mental phenomena in relation to the rest of reality; that is to say, they concern the *metaphysical* status of mental phenomena. And it is with such questions that this book will be in large part, although by no means exclusively, occupied.

How is philosophy of mind, which is today often called

philosophical psychology, related to psychology as an empirical science? The former has as its primary responsibility the *analysis* of the *concepts* of consciousness and specific mental phenomena. The latter has as its primary responsibility the *empirical investigation* of the *phenomena* these concepts refer to, rather than the conceptual investigation of the concepts themselves. Take memory, for example: the philosopher asks what it *means* to say of someone that he remembers something or that he forgets something, how the *concept* of remembering and the *concept* of forgetting are related, how both are related to learning, knowing, the past, and such *concepts*. On the other hand, the psychologist studies the *phenomena* of memory, actual instances in which someone remembers or forgets something, under what circumstances things are remembered best or forgotten most easily, the effects of age, practice, and reward on memory, and so on. This is not to say that the two fields have no connections. The understanding of concepts may require certain sorts of empirical knowledge. And one cannot go out and study the phenomena of memory unless one has some idea what to look for, which is to say, some idea of what the word "memory" means, some idea of what the concept of memory is. So these two fields progress best when their practitioners work with some acquaintance of each other's results.

What is consciousness?   To say that the crucial concept in the philosophy of mind is consciousness (see page 4) does not take us very far. For it still remains for us to say what this consciousness is. One thing we can say about consciousness is this: it is something which distinguishes man from a good deal of the world around him. Even if some of the higher animals are conscious too, it is still the case that it is a great rarity, as can be seen when we consider the absence of it over large portions of the earth's surface, in most of the earth's interior, and in most of the enormous spaces surrounding the earth. It would not be surprising if consciousness occurred in other places in the vastness of the universe, but wherever it occurs it probably is possessed by a minuscule proportion of the things that exist. It is possessed by only the living, not by the dead which once lived nor by the inorganic which never lived. And even among the living it is not found in the plants or in the lower forms of animal life; amoebae, for example, do not seem to be conscious. As we go up the ladder of living animals, it becomes harder to say. Jellyfish? Oysters? Ants? Flies? Bats? Goldfish? Frogs? Snakes? Cows? Owls? Tigers? Dogs? Chimpanzees? Could we draw a line dividing those who have consciousness from those who do not? Probably not.

Some philosophers have reasoned from the fact that inorganic material is clearly nonconscious and the fact that we cannot draw a line between the nonconscious and the conscious to the conclusion that the higher forms of life, including man, are not conscious either. Other philosophers have reasoned from the fact that man is conscious and the fact that we cannot draw a line to the conclusion that even the inorganic forms of existence are conscious. Both arguments are fallacious, however. It would be like arguing from the fact that we cannot draw a line in the spectrum where blue ends and green begins to the conclusion that the whole blue-green part of the spectrum is really blue on the one hand or really green on the other. That we cannot draw a sharp dividing line does not mean there is no difference between the extremes. That there is a difference between the nonconscious and the conscious is an undeniable fact and the starting point of our inquiry.

Our inquiry arises with the question, "What is consciousness?" What is this something which man certainly has, rocks and amoebae certainly lack, and frogs and snakes perhaps have?

In trying to answer this question, let us start by examining an actual instance of consciousness and see if we can notice what is going on. Stare at something on this page, some word, for example, making yourself conscious of its form and character. Now try to notice what your *consciousness* of that word is. What do you get? Perhaps you will find that all you observe is the *word* on the paper and not the *consciousness* of the word on the paper. As G. E. Moore wrote (using a blue patch as his object of consciousness): "The moment we try to fix our attention upon consciousness and to see *what*, distinctly, it is, it seems to vanish: it seems as if we had before us a mere emptiness. When we try to introspect the sensation of blue, all we can see is the blue: the other element is as if it were diaphanous." [2] This, I think, is the result that most of us would get when we try this experiment. Yet, of course, we know perfectly well we are conscious of the word on the page. What is this consciousness?

The nineteenth century psychologist G. T. Ladd characterized consciousness in this way: "What we are when we are awake, as contrasted with what we are when we sink into a profound and perfectly dreamless sleep, or receive an overpowering blow upon the head—*that* it is to be conscious. What we are less and less as we sink gradually down into dreamless sleep, or as we swoon slowly away: and what we are more and more, as the noise of the crowd outside momentarily arouses us from our after-dinner nap, or as we

[2] G. E. Moore, *Philosophical Studies* (London: Routledge & Kegan Paul, Ltd., 1922), p. 25.

come out of the midnight darkness of the typhoid-fever crisis—*that it is to become conscious.*" [3]

We find it so difficult to say what consciousness is because there is such an enormous *variety* of phenomena which could plausibly be said to involve consciousness, and within each variety can be found great complexity. For example, one would not want to say that a stone could have beliefs; only a conscious being could have beliefs. Yet when I fall into a deep and dreamless sleep, do I cease to have beliefs? Do I lose all my beliefs every night and regain them in the morning? Of course not. And even when I am wide awake, fully conscious, I may not be conscious of any of my beliefs. In fact, there might be beliefs that I hold but have *never* been conscious of, perhaps never will be conscious of in my entire life. A person may feel ashamed of himself whenever he gets sick but never realize that he is ashamed because he happens to believe that getting sick indicates that he is *inferior*. Now, let us contrast believing with being in considerable pain. This, too, involves consciousness; a stone could not feel pain. Yet it would not make sense to say of a man in a deep and dreamless sleep that he was in considerable pain, nor would it make sense to say of a man that all his life he had considerable pain of which he was *never* conscious. Why should one think there is some common "conscious" element present both in beliefs and sensations, making both of them phenomena of consciousness? No wonder one would be baffled if he tried to say what that "common" element is. Consider dreams. A person may be lying perfectly still, impervious to his environment, showing no signs of consciousness, and yet he may be having extraordinarily vivid dream imagery. Contrast this mode of consciousness with concentrating on some activity like hunting; here one is totally aware of one's environment and sensitive to every change. What could one say about the "common" element here? Or consider states of mind. A person who is preoccupied may be lost in thought, daydreams, reveries; a person who is agitated is given to rapid and incomplete movements. The essence of the one seems to lie in inner events; the essence of the other seems to lie in outward events. Could we hope to find a significant common denominator here?

As for complexity, very few concepts isolate purely mental phenomena. Consider memory. Many things may happen to a stone, but a stone cannot *remember* what happened to it (although it may bear traces of what happened to it). But to remember something is much more complex than simply to be in some mental state. Even

---

[3] *Psychology, Descriptive and Explanatory* (1894), p. 30.

where there is some mental state—e.g., the presence of an image of one's former home—that is not enough for it to be a memory. One must have certain *beliefs*, e.g., that it is an image of his former home. Certain nonmental conditions must obtain, such as that one did in fact live in such a home; and certain conditions which are a combination of mental and nonmental conditions must obtain—e.g., that one's present image is not a result of having seen a picture of his former home but is a result of having seen the home itself. Finally, the presence of an image is not even necessary. One can be said to remember his former home even if he does not have any image at all, but simply picks it out from other houses as he drives through the neighborhood.

Some theories of mental phenomena   Because of the variety and complexity of mental phenomena, it is not surprising that philosophers should have disagreed violently on what characterizes the essence of the mind and of consciousness. Some philosophers have concentrated on our various capacities to know and reason things out, and they have concluded that the essential feature of the mind is *rationality*. This is reflected even in the name of our species, Homo sapiens, the Intelligent Man. Others have concentrated on our capacities to conjure up images, have thoughts, feel sensations, and experience emotions, and they have concluded that the essence of the mind lies in its *contemplative awareness* of a special kind of inner and private object. There are those philosophers who stress the typically human activities of reporting, reminiscing, judging, arguing, inventing, pretending, and imitating, in the view that the essence of the mind lies in its ability to *symbolize, form abstractions,* and *use language*. Finally, some have been struck by the fact that thinking, believing, desiring, expecting, hoping, intending and looking for, among others, have *objects* which can be thought about, believed, desired, expected, etc., even if these objects do not actually exist at all (one can think about a unicorn even if there happen not to be any unicorns). Using the word "intentional" to mark the peculiar status of such objects, these philosophers characterize mental phenomena as those including an object "intentionally" within themselves.

One cannot help thinking here of the story of the blind men and the elephant, for each of these theories of the essence of the mind depends for its plausibility upon a limited sample of examples. For its own limited sample, each theory does pick out an important feature, but each theory succeeds only by ignoring other phenomena that fit one of the rival theories better. At best, each theory picks out a sufficient condition for mentality, but not a necessary condition.

We have, in the case of mental phenomena, a vast range of phenomena overlapping in various ways without having any one essence in common. We may say, using Wittgenstein's concept, that we have here a "family" of items in which the members bear a "family resemblance," like the members of a family who may all resemble one another, even though they have no one feature (e.g., the shape of the nose) in common.[4]

It might even be questioned here whether we have a genuine family at all constituting a kind of things to be called mental phenomena or minds. Admittedly, stones cannot dream, whereas humans can; but stones cannot float in salt water, whereas humans can; and no one would want to say that floating in salt water is a "mental phenomenon." The higher mammals have many things that the rest of nature lacks, such as a particular sort of metabolism, but there is nothing peculiarly "mental" about a particular sort of metabolism. If we remember our earlier characterization of mental phenomena as phenomena that can characterize only a subject capable of consciousness, then we would have to include many things not usually thought of as particularly mental. For example, all of the following require that the subject is conscious: stuttering, scowling, getting a divorce, missing a putt. Yet are they *mental* phenomena?

In reply it must be admitted that we are somewhat stretching the word "mental" here, but usefully, we believe. Stuttering, for example, is not the mere physical production of certain noises—a steam engine could not be said, except metaphorically, to stutter. Stuttering must be understood against a background of *conscious* beings using a language with particular intentions. Scowling is not the mere play of certain facial muscles; it can be understood only in the context of *feelings* of displeasure or disapproval. We cannot make sense of these phenomena if we ignore the fact that their subjects are conscious beings. And to that extent they deserve to be considered in the same class with other phenomena that are, admittedly, more central to the nature of conscious beings.

In the following chapters we will develop in more detail the central issues in the philosophy of mind. The problem of Chapter 2

---

[4] The notion that a group of things may not have a common essence but may still have a "family resemblance" is developed by Ludwig Wittgenstein in *Philosophical Investigations*, trans. G. E. M. Anscombe (New York: The Macmillan Company, 1953, second edition, 1958), secs. 66-71.

is whether consciousness in any of its various manifestations is a private, inner phenomenon accessible only to the subject himself or whether it is essentially a public phenomenon as observable by others as by the subject himself. In Chapter 3, we will examine *what* it is that can be said to be conscious, and we will consider three alternatives: the body, the mind, and the person. Chapter 4 deals with the traditional mind-body problem and the questions of an afterlife and psychic phenomena. Chapter 5 concerns consciousness as it is expressed in our intentional actions.

CONSCIOUSNESS

2

If we were to survey the various theories about *consciousness* that have been proposed in the twenty-five hundred years of known work, we would find that they fall into two general patterns. There is what we shall call the first-person account, which results from attending to how things are *in one's own case*. And there is the third-person account, which results from attending to how things are when *someone else* is conscious in some way. I take these terms from grammar; one typically uses the grammatical first-person to say things about *oneself* and one typically uses the grammatical third-person to say things about *others*. (We could call these the "subjective" and "objective" account, respectively, except that these terms are currently used in so many different ways that we would run the risk of introducing irrelevant considerations.) These approaches yield quite different accounts of consciousness.

The third-person account When we ask of a man who has been hit on the head whether he is *conscious*, what do we mean? Well, what do we expect to find if we are told he is not conscious, and what do we expect to find if we are told that he is conscious? We expect that if he is not conscious, he will not respond to certain stimuli; for example, he will not flinch at a loud noise nearby. On the other hand, we expect that if he is conscious, he will flinch at the noise. That is, we expect certain kinds of behavior under certain stimuli. For example, we expect he will open his eyes when he is spoken to, perhaps try to get up, ask what happened to him, and so on. If he has not suffered bodily injury, then we will expect even more complex behavior. If, on request, he is able to get up, walk around without bumping into things, reply to questions, follow commands, then it would be absurd for anyone to wonder if he is conscious yet. Just that kind of behavior is exactly the sort of behavior we have in mind when we say that a person has regained consciousness. This fact might lead us to say that "consciousness" is to be defined in terms of the kind of bodily behavior elicited by certain sorts of stimuli. Such a definition would fall under the heading of what is usually called behaviorism.

Behaviorism has played an important role in recent psychology. It was adopted as the label for a major movement in twentieth century psychology, and most psychologists today are greatly indebted to it. Unfortunately, they have often failed to make a distinction between two forms of it, which may be called methodological behaviorism and metaphysical behaviorism. The former is a method of approach to problems in the field of psychology; it consists in confining psychological theories and the procedures for evaluating those theories to observable behavior. Such a method of approach has been highly fruitful in dealing with problems in the field of psychology. Metaphysical behaviorism is a theory about the *nature* of consciousness and the *analysis* of expressions referring to consciousness. It is metaphysical, not methodological, behaviorism that concerns us here.

Behaviorism is a typical third-person account since it proposes that we define all expressions involving consciousness in terms of bodily behavior which can be observed in *others* as easily as in oneself. But such a view must be carefully formulated, since it is obvious that a person who is conscious or who is in some particular conscious state may not be behaving in any noticeable way. He may just be flat on his back, eyes shut. Yet he may still be conscious, having sensations and thoughts, and so on. He may be in pain, for example, without writhing, groaning, complaining. How is the behaviorist to take this into account in his theory?

For one thing, the behaviorist may hold that *future* behavior is relevant; for example, what a person will write in his diary tonight, what he will confess under torture tomorrow, what he will say on his deathbed. But it is clear that this is not sufficient, for the person in pain now may *never show* future behavior appropriate to his being in pain now.

Some behaviorists distinguish between *overt* and *covert* behavior, the latter being movements that are not noticed, either because they are so very slight or because they occur inside the body where they cannot be observed very easily. Thus, thinking, for example, can be associated with very slight movements of the lips or, more plausibly, with slight movements of the tongue or vocal chords. However, this attempt to evade the difficulty raises new difficulties. First: recent work with the drug curare, which produces temporary paralysis, indicates that even covert behavior may be absent during mental events. Patients with enough curare to produce complete muscular paralysis report, after the drug has worn off, that there is no absence of consciousness, thoughts, sensations, ability to think, images, or the like, during the paralysis. So it may not be possible to identify mental events with behavior in any sense, either overt or covert. Second: suppose we did find certain slight muscular movements in the vocal cords when people think. Could it possibly be argued that when we say of someone that he just had a thought, we *mean* by those words something about muscular movements in his vocal cords? Surely not. One could fully understand such a remark without the slightest knowledge of the muscles of the vocal chords. So it is not very likely that the meanings of mentalistic terms can be analyzed in terms of actual behavior.

A typical behavioristic device for dealing with the fact that a person in a particular mental state may not be behaving in any particular way is to introduce the concept of a *disposition to behave.* Dispositions are properties of things such that under certain circumstances the thing that has the dispositional property will undergo a certain change. For example, brittleness is a dispositional property: a thing is brittle if, and only if, under suitable circumstances it will shatter. An object may have the dispositional property of brittleness and still never shatter; that is why we handle brittle objects with care. It is because of this feature of dispositional properties that the behaviorist can use them in his analysis. For if we define thoughts, feelings, wishes, etc., in terms not of behavior but of dispositions to behave, then the man who hides his thoughts, feelings, and wishes behind a poker face and poker behavior would still have *dispositions* to behave in certain ways. So to attribute consciousness or some particular state of consciousness is to attribute a disposition to behave in particular ways.

There is a difficulty here, however, when we come to ask *what* dispositions are involved? Consider the man who is conscious. What dispositions are we to attribute to him? We might say, for a start, that part of what is involved is a disposition to answer questions.

But it is clear that a man may be conscious without being disposed to answer questions. He may be concentrating on something so much that he does not even hear the questions; he may not understand the language; he may not wish to answer questions; he may not be physically capable of answering questions. And, in general, no matter how elaborately we described the conditions under which the disposition would result in behavior, one could still imagine cases where the behavior would not be forthcoming even though the man was fully conscious. So it looks as though the behaviorist's claim cannot be substantiated; we cannot provide even the beginning of an analysis in terms of dispositions to behave.

But the behaviorist is not daunted by this difficulty. He will argue that, although we may not be able to pin down the relevant dispositions to behave, nevertheless we all have a rough idea of the kind of behavior that is relevant. Or else *how could we ever tell when someone is conscious?* After all, it is only behavior that we have to go by. Given enough behavior of the right sort, we can establish that a person is conscious. And it is the behaviorist's proposal that such behavior, even if it cannot be explicitly described, *constitutes* being conscious.

In support of the behaviorist a *general* feature of dispositional terms must be acknowledged: we can never spell out in detail what will happen under various conditions to things that have the disposition, because indefinitely many unforeseeable complexities could interfere with realization of the disposition. This fact, not the incorrectness of his thesis, creates difficulty for the behaviorist, so his failure to provide an actual dispositional analysis cannot be held against him.

The merit of the third-person account   Now it must be said at the outset that this third-person account does indeed do considerable justice to a great many of the concepts applicable exclusively to conscious beings. If we say of a person that he is ingenious or witty, resourceful or industrious, ambitious or considerate, we are referring predominantly to what he says and does. And the same goes for knowing Latin, reminiscing, studying the behavior of a cat, and flying into a rage. The crucial tests for the application of these terms and, indeed, their basic content, lie in behavior and behavioral dispositions.[1]

For example, *to know Latin* is to be able to perform in pre-

---

[1] It is one of the great merits of Gilbert Ryle's *The Concept of Mind* (New York: Barnes and Noble, 1949) that he demonstrates this thesis over and over for an astonishing range of expressions involving a reference to consciousness.

scribed ways under certain circumstances. At the very least, one must be able to translate a goodly number of sentences into and out of Latin, and it is even better if one can explain *why* he uses the constructions he does. *To be greedy* is to jump at opportunities to increase one's acquisitions, or at least be strongly inclined to jump at them, far beyond actual need. And *to exercise reason* or *intelligence* is to do things in sensible and efficacious ways, avoiding pitfalls and surmounting obstacles with a minimum of effort.

It might be said in general that the third-person account is applicable to what can be classified as qualities of mind, personality and character, of skills, abilities and capacities (or the absence thereof), of habits, tendencies, propensities and bents, of attitudes and outlooks, and of moods, frames of mind and humors; and to whatever is an exercise or expression of them.

Why is it that the third-person account is especially applicable to the analysis of these concepts? It is no accident. This can be seen when we ask what entitles someone to apply any one of these concepts to himself. Consider, for example, knowing Latin. *My* opinion that I know Latin has no special weight, balanced against another's opinion. Anyone who claims I know Latin must have *evidence*, and that includes me. The kind of evidence that is relevant is the kind that not only I but anyone could have. So others are typically in as good a position as I am to say of me that I know Latin. In the case of some concepts, such as *ambition*, others often are in an even better position to know, for they may look more objectively at my behavior than I do.

The fact that, in principle, I am in no better position to describe my own state indicates that even when I do describe my state, I take an essentially *third-person* approach to myself, taking account of the sorts of things any third person would when he makes a judgment. So the third-person account would be naturally well suited to the analysis of such states and would furnish an appropriate analysis.

Note that even for the concepts most amenable to behavioristic analysis, it is out of the question that we should be able to give a precise dispositional *definition*. We cannot say in detail just what dispositions are involved. From that fact, some would conclude that the third-person account is inadequate even here. But a supporter of that account would remind us that this is a general feature of dispositional terms.

Whether the third-person account does justice to all of the concepts involving consciousness remains to be seen. Let us turn to a set of cases notorious for the difficulties they offer to a proponent of the third-person account.

Some difficulties in the third-person account We may bring out the important feature of such cases by noting a peculiarity of cases favorable to the third-person account, cases such as knowing Latin or being ambitious. It may very well be true of a person who is *sound asleep* that he knows Latin or is greedy; it is not necessary that there be anything, as we say, *going on before his mind* or *occupying his consciousness*. When it comes to the exercise or expression of these states, he must, typically, be awake (I say "typically," because one might argue that a person speaking Latin in his sleep is exercising his knowledge of Latin, and the person crying out in his sleep "I want the whole cake!" is giving expression to his greed). Although it is not easy to see this point, reflection will show that it is not necessary even in the standard case of being awake that there be anything particular *going on before his mind or occupying his consciousness* when he gives expression to his knowledge of Latin or his greed. He may recite a Latin poem automatically or reach out and grab the whole cake on impulse, without any thought. To be sure, he *might* be inwardly reciting the poem in addition to reciting it outwardly, and he *might* be inwardly enjoying the thought of eating the whole cake as he grabs it. But such inward experiences are not essential. The essence of the expression of the knowledge or the greed consists in what is done *outwardly*, not what is done *inwardly*.

To find cases that offer difficulty to the third-person account, we must look for those cases in which the essence lies in what happens *inwardly*. It is the thesis of adherents of the third-person account that there are *no* such cases, that anything involving consciousness can be analyzed in terms of publicly observable behavior or dispositions toward such behavior.

Let us turn to those cases in which it appears that an essential feature of the case is the *inner* occurrence of something, as we say, "going on before the person's mind" or "occupying his consciousness." The most plausible candidates are sensations (e.g., feeling pain), mental images (e.g., visualizing a scene), and thoughts (e.g., having the thought, upon awakening, that today is a holiday). Let us concentrate on having sensations; for example, a *sensation of pain*. We see a heavy object fall on someone's foot. We see him turn pale, grimace, cry out, clutch his foot, jump up and down, call for help, and limp about. He is obviously feeling pain. But what is it to feel pain? On the third-person account it is just to behave in these ways under these circumstances, or at least to be disposed so to behave. That is all that is observable in principle, and so that is all that is involved in feeling pain.

But does not such an analysis leave out just the essential feature, the sharp, highly unpleasant *sensation* so forcibly there in the forefront of consciousness and so agonizingly distressful? Surely it is the inner sensation which is the immediate cause of the outward behavior of grimacing, crying out, and limping about. That inner cause is left out in the third-person account. Particular behavior or dispositions to behave are neither necessary nor sufficient conditions for sensations. Not necessary because one can imagine a pain so paralyzingly great or so trivially slight that there is no disposition to behave; and one can imagine stoics who have so trained themselves that they have exterminated any such dispositions. And not sufficient because one can imagine such dispositions arising from other causes such as the desire to call attention to oneself, to deceive others, or imitate a person in pain; and you can imagine even that suddenly and unaccountably you might be overcome by a desire to grimace, cry out, and limp about, *for no reason at all.* Such an occurrence would be very puzzling, and we might not know what to make of it, but surely it might occur. Others might be taken in and believe that you were feeling pain. But *you* would know that you were not feeling pain, even if you could not explain *why* you behaved as though you were in pain. So feeling pain is one thing, and being disposed to behave in certain ways is another. The feeling may produce the disposition to behave, but we cannot say they are identical, nor even that the one is a necessary or sufficient condition for the other.

One might try to deal with this objection by broadening the definition of sensations beyond behavior. One way in which this might be done while still remaining consistent with the third-person account is to bring into the picture a publicly observable *cause*; e.g., the heavy object falling on his foot and causing his disposition to grimace, cry out, and limp around. We can define the feeling of pain as the disposition to behave in the revelant ways *as a result of* a particular sort of injury to the body. In this way, we would rule out those cases in which the disposition to behave is caused by a desire (e.g., to imitate a person in pain) or in which the disposition to behave has no known cause at all.

The difficulty with this attempt to bolster the third-person account is that it makes the cause a part of the *definition* of "sensation," and the proposition that every sensation has a cause becomes a tautology. But it is clearly *not* a tautology that every sensation has a cause; it is an empirical hypothesis. Since speaking of a sensation without any cause is not a contradiction in terms, this suggested analysis, which would make it a contradiction, must be rejected.

A way of getting around this difficulty is proposed by David K. Lewis.[2] He suggests that we define the sensation in terms of its typical causes and effects, and admit that there may be a small residue of atypical cases. This suggestion, however, commits us to the view that the proposition that *most sensations have causes* is a tautology. And I am inclined to think that even though it is highly likely, perhaps even certain, that most sensations have causes, it is not a tautology. Take headaches, for instance; is it not logically possible that they should occur randomly? That most headaches have causes is surely an empirical hypothesis. Hence we cannot bring in their causes, not even typical causes, to define the term "headache."

I conclude, then, that such third-person accounts will not give us a correct account of mental events such as sensations. There seems to be a purely contingent connection between such mental events and their causal antecedents, their behavioral effects, and even behavioral dispositions. And therefore the third-person account, as broadened, still will not do as an analysis of consciousness. Let us then turn to the alternative, the first-person account.

The first-person account   So far we have sought to define consciousness in third-person terms, in terms of what we can observe of others. We have treated consciousness as if it were simply a public and objective phenomenon like porousness, radioactivity, or brittleness, for example, which we learn about through observation. And this has forced us to restrict ourselves in our understanding of consciousness to behavior and dispositions to behave, and observable causes of behavior, since these are the sorts of things that, typically, *show* that another is conscious and, anyhow, these are the *only* sorts of things that can be observed of consciousness in others.

But we have overlooked a most obvious but important fact, one that a supporter of the first-person account would wish to remind us of: *we ourselves* are conscious, too, not just others. Therefore, in trying to understand what consciousness is, we do not have to restrict ourselves to what we can observe in *others*. It is the thesis of the adherents of the first-person account that we can learn what consciousness is *from our own case*. If each of us turns his attention inward to what is going on in himself when he is conscious, then

[2] "An Argument for the Identity Theory," *The Journal of Philosophy*, LXIII, No. 1 (January 6, 1966), 17–25, esp. 22.

he will see that being conscious is not a matter of behaving in particular (viz., conscious) ways; the behavior is merely the outward manifestation of the inner state. *Because* I am conscious, my behavior demonstrates consciousness. And this inner consciousness is there to be observed by me in my own case.

On the first-person account, we can learn what consciousness is from our own case. Thus, when we wake up in the morning from a deep, dreamless sleep, we can notice the presence of a state qualitatively different from what went on before; that new state is what it is to be conscious. When we open our eyes we can notice we are conscious of colors and shapes; that is what it is to be visually conscious. When a thorn pierces our skin, we can notice that we are having an unpleasant sensation; that is what it is to have a sensation of pain. When we are insulted, we are conscious of a rising sensation of anger; that is what it is to have an emotional feeling. When we remember that during the night we had various sorts of imagery, we know what it is to have a dream. When it suddenly flashes through our mind that some statement is true, we know what it is to have a thought. Recalling something, having an afterimage, forming an intention, making a decision, adding in one's head, and the rest of our conscious states—in all these, we learn what the state is not by careful observation of others but by experiencing the state ourselves. Then we learn which words to affix to which states; and that is to come to understand what the expressions referring to those states *mean*. The adherents of the first-person account might put their thesis in this way: we come to understand the meanings of such expressions as "is conscious," "has a sensation of pain," "feels angry," etc., by having the inner experience and learning to affix the right word to inner experiences of that kind.

The thesis of
Intentionality

There is a school of philosophy called phenomenology which holds that the inner nature of consciousness—the thing G. E. Moore referred to as "diaphanous"—can be studied and its nature can be elucidated by careful examination. This school was founded by the German philosopher Edmund Husserl at the beginning of this century, and the bulk of its followers are still located in Europe (although there is a strong and, indeed, growing interest in it here in North America). Husserl held that:

> We are accustomed to concentrate upon the matters, thoughts, and values of the moment, and not upon the psychical "act of experience" in which these are apprehended. This "act" is revealed

by a "reflection"; and a reflection can be practised on every experience. Instead of the matters themselves, the values, goals, utilities, etc., we regard the subjective experiences in which these "appear." [3]

If I reflect properly on my states of consciousness (and Husserl offers a number of rules to be followed in doing this), I will be "learning thus what is the nature of the psychical, and comprehending the being of the soul," and when I follow this procedure to the very end, "I am face to face at last with the ultimate structure of consciousness."[4]

Husserl and his followers offer many careful and elaborate descriptions of various states of consciousness; however, when it comes to giving a general characterization of consciousness, they fall back on a thesis maintained by an earlier thinker, Franz Brentano. Brentano was not himself a phenomenologist, although he was a teacher of Husserl's and exerted a powerful influence in the development of that movement.

Brentano noticed that consciousness is not merely contrasted with unconsciousness; we also speak of being conscious *of* this or that, as in "He was conscious of the tingling in his scalp." It was Brentano's claim that consciousness was always consciousness *of* something, that it always was *about* something and *directed toward* that something. It was this *aboutness* which he held to be the essential characteristic of consciousness; any mental state must have this characteristic, and no physical state could have it.

Brentano's claim, now called the thesis of intentionality, is very much a matter of contemporary controversy.[5] Many philosophers believe that this feature of "aboutness" is neither a necessary nor a sufficient condition of consciousness.[6] For the purposes of our present discussion, however, it is sufficient to note that nothing here helps us so far as the issue between the third-person account and the first-person account is concerned. For even if the thesis of intentionality is correct, this question remains: What is the nature of "aboutness"? And there are those who will say that the meaning of, for example, "thinking about his childhood in Nebraska" is to be

---

[3] Edmund Husserl, "Phenomenology," *Encyclopaedia Britannica,* 14th ed., 1929, as reprinted in Roderick M. Chisholm, *Realism and the Background of Phenomenology* (New York: The Free Press, 1960), p. 119.

[4] *Ibid.,* pp. 120, 125.

[5] Brentano's statement can be found in Chisholm, ed., *Realism and the Background of Phenomenology,* pp. 39-61. It is elaborated and defended in Chisholm's *Perceiving* (Ithaca, N.Y.: Cornell University Press, 1957), Chap. 11.

[6] See, e.g., Herbert Heidelberger, "On Characterizing the Psychological," *Philosophy and Phenomenological Research,* XXVI, No. 4 (1966), 529-36.

explained in terms of behavior or dispositions to behave; and there are those who will say that its meaning can be given only by an introspective examination conducted by the person who himself is in that state. So whether the thesis is true or false, it does not help us settle between the two accounts we are here exploring.

The private ostensive definition   It is a crucial part of the first-person account that we must learn what states of consciousness are, what expressions referring to states of consciousness mean, by what is sometimes called *private ostensive definition*.

An "ostensive definition" consists in explaining the meaning of an expression to someone by giving him a series of examples of the things to which the expression refers. To explain to someone what color-words like "red," "green," and "yellow," mean, we would give him examples of red, green, and yellow things until he caught on to the meanings of these terms. It is frequently held, and most plausibly, too, that it is only by means of ostensive definition that the meanings of such expressions can be learned; it would be most unlikely, to say the least, that a person who had never seen colored objects (for example, a person blind from birth) would know fully what color-words mean. I say "fully" because it is possible that a congenitally blind person have *some* grasp of the meaning. He may know the grammar of such words, use them correctly in many situations, and even have some idea of their content. John Locke tells the following story:

> A studious blind man, who had mightily beat his head about visible objects, and made use of the explication of his books and friends to understand those names of light and colours which often came in his way, bragged one day, that he now understood what scarlet signified. Upon which his friend demanding, what scarlet was? The blind man answered, It was like the sound of a trumpet.[7]

Now that is not bad, considering the man was blind. But if it is the best he could do, then it is still a long way from understanding the meaning of "scarlet." And Locke himself, a leading spokesman for the first-person account, concluded that until the man actually experiences scarlet, he can never come to understand the meaning of the word.

A supporter of the first-person account holds that at least some sensation-words *must* be learned by ostensive definition, by being

[7] *An Essay Concerning Human Understanding*, III, iv, 11.

presented with examples of particular sensations. But examples of someone else's sensation are inadequate for learning the meanings of these words. The person *himself* must have the sensation. A person who, for example, never had experienced pain (there are people with abnormal nervous systems that render them incapable of feeling pain; their lives are filled with danger because of it) would not fully understand expressions like "pain," "ache," or "twinge" on this account. He would presumably know that they dispose people to behave in certain ways, and so he would have the kind of understanding of these expressions that the third-person account supplies. But this would be an inadequate understanding, as we noted when we considered the difficulties in the third-person account.

Since the person himself must experience the sensation, to come to learn the full meaning of the sensation-word, the example he is presented with is not one that another could use for learning the full meaning. It is a "private" example, and the ostensive definition is a "private" ostensive definition. On the first-person account, this element of "privacy" is an essential part of the meanings of sensation-words. The situation is quite different for words like "curved" or "horse"; the referents of these words are public in that more than one person could observe the referents and use them to learn the meanings of those words. But if a person feels pain, only *he* can have *that* feeling; others may feel their own pain, but they cannot feel his. They may be able to tell from the situation and his behavior that he is in pain, but they cannot tell *by feeling* his pain. His pain is private to himself; no one else can feel it. Anything any other person feels will be that other person's feeling.

An objection The presence of this important element, the private ostensive definition, in the first-person account has prompted a serious objection to that account, raised by the late Ludwig Wittgenstein and his followers. Wittgenstein argued that if one holds that the initial application of expressions involving consciousness is to oneself, if one learns the meanings of these expressions by a private ostensive definition, then insoluble difficulties arise concerning the application of such expressions to *others*.

Two such difficulties are these. First, there is the problem of verification; namely, could we ever have any *grounds* for applying them to others? After all, we can never observe another's inner sensation; we can do that only in our own case. All we can observe, so far as others are concerned, is their *outward behavior*. So could we ever be entitled to say of another that he has the inner sensation?

This is a particular case of the general problem known as the problem of other minds: how can I know, or even have the slightest reason to believe, that inner states of what I know as consciousness in my own case ever occur in any case other than my own? We shall consider this problem later on, but it can be said at this point that it is a most difficult problem, and none of the proposed solutions turns out to be very satisfactory.

But there is another problem here concerning how such expressions, which get their meanings from what I experience in my own case, could apply to others. This is not the problem of verification, but the prior problem of *meaning*. How could it be even intelligible to attribute *that which I feel* to another? Suppose I am to attribute a pain in the foot to that man. On the first-person account it would be to attribute to that foot what I feel in my own case. But what is such an attribution? Is it to assert the existence of a pain that I feel but that is somehow *located* in that foot over there? If so, it would be a case in which I feel a pain in someone else's foot. But that is obviously not what is meant when I attribute a pain in the foot to that man. I must attribute to that foot a pain which is like what I feel *but which is not felt by me at all*. And if what I experience in my own case is so essentially something felt by me, how can I understand an expression that attributes a sensation to another, in which that something felt by me is claimed to be something not felt by me at all? If, by "in pain," I mean something felt by me, how can I talk about pain (another's) not felt by me?[8]

What is needed here is a distinction between my pain and another person's pain. The first-person account does not allow for such a distinction. Since the meaning of sensation words is given by what *I* feel, a sensation that is somehow like what I feel but unfelt by me would be utterly impossible, on the first-person account. If I learn that "pain" means *this which is now felt*, then if I feel no pain, there is no pain at all to be felt, and that is the end of the matter. The first-person account allows distinctions between different sorts of sensations (e.g., tickles, itches, pains) and between past, present, and future sensations (via memories and expectations), but it does not allow a distinction between sensations that are mine and sensations that are another's. And no private ostensive definition *could* be used to teach the distinction between *my* sensation and *another's*.

One might be inclined to think that such a distinction would

[8] This is pointed out by Wittgenstein in *Philosophical Investigations*, trans. G. E. M. Anscombe (New York: The Macmillan Company, 1953), sec. 302.

be easy to make. After all, it might be argued, if I know what pain that *I* feel is, what could be easier to imagine than a pain that another feels? But this way of putting it conceals the basic difficulty. For I do not learn the "my pain" vs. "his pain" contrast by attending to what happens in my own case. From my own case I learn only such contrasts as "pain" vs. "tickle," on the one hand, and "pain" vs. "no pain" on the other.

Since it is an essential part of our concepts of sensations and of consciousness in general that it be intelligible to apply them to others, we must conclude that the first-person account does not succeed in explaining how we have such concepts and how the words standing for such concepts come to be meaningful.

Because of this problem with the first-person account as well as the problem of verification mentioned above, some philosophers have said that when one attributes to *oneself* a state of consciousness, he attributes an inner state; but when one attributes to *another* a state of consciousness, *he attributes only behavior.* Thus, when I say of myself that I am in pain, I am attributing the sensation; but when I say of another that he is in pain, I am attributing a disposition to display pain behavior; e.g., groaning, thrashing about, and so on.

This compromise between the third-person account and the first-person account is a desperate compromise indeed. For it asserts a radical difference in the meaning of the expression "in pain" when it occurs in "I am in pain" and in "He is in pain." But this is to introduce intolerable complexities into the language. What are we to make of "He and I [i.e., we] are in pain"? And when another says of me, "He is in pain," and I "agree" with him that I am in pain, what am I *agreeing* to, the ascription of the sensation or the ascription of a behavioral disposition? Similarly, when I say I am in pain, and another believes what I say, how is he to express his belief and what is he to mean by the words expressing that belief? Is his belief about my inner sensation or my outer behavior?

So far as our language is concerned, at least, "in pain" is treated as having the same meaning whether it is used to apply to oneself or to another. When one reports the occurrence of a pain, whether it is in oneself or in another, one intends to report the occurrence of one and the same thing and one uses the expression "in pain" as meaning one and the same thing. The question is, What is one to mean, inner sensation or outer behavior?

On the first-person account, we end up meaning *our own* inner sensations. Our problem has been how to attribute inner sensation to second and third parties. We have considered the view that we mean inner sensations in our own case but outward behavior in the case of others, and we have found that it introduces an intolerable asymmetry into our language, something to be avoided if possible.

A compromise
solution To summarize so far, neither of the two accounts we have examined gives an adequate account of consciousness, and yet each brings out an important facet. The obvious solution is to try to see what is true and correct in each of the two accounts, noticing that it is essential to the nature of consciousness that there be *both* a first-person and a third-person aspect. The difficulty lies in seeing how the two are related. In the main, this is the task of the next chapter. But certain important relations can be pointed out here without begging any of the issues of Chapter 3.

Let us consider how we learn and teach others to use expressions involving a reference to consciousness. I do not mean here to get into questions of empirical psychology, questions concerning how, in fact, children come to possess the ability to use these expressions. I mean to ask what sorts of thing would we *call* "teaching" and "learning" here. The following would be a case: The child stubs his toe and cries; I say "It hurts, doesn't it?" The child says "It hurts." Thereafter, when he stubs his toe, he says "It hurts." I think we would all say that here is a case of teaching and learning the meaning of the expression "It hurts." From the teacher's point of view, what is essential is that there be (1) the causal conditions of stubbing the toe and the behavioral response of crying and (2) subsequent similar conditions and response plus the new behavior of uttering the expression "It hurts." The first shows that it is an appropriate teaching situation, and the second shows that learning took place. From the learner's point of view, what is essential is (1) that he pick out the element in the situation referred to by "It hurts" and (2) that he associate similar occurrences of that element with the expression.

I think we would all agree that here is a case of teaching and learning the meaning of the expression "It hurts." It must be noted, however, that it is not *inevitable* that anything correct be taught and learned in such a case. It is possible that the child might fail to pick out the correct element in the situation referred to by "It hurts," even though he goes on to use the expression in the appropriate future circumstances. It is possible, but it is not usual or typical of these cases. If it did happen frequently that the person failed to pick out the correct element and still did somehow go on to use the expression in the appropriate circumstances, then this sort of case would *not* be a case of teaching and learning the meaning of the expression "It hurts." But it is a fact that typically the correct element is picked out. And that is what makes it a case of teaching and learning the meaning of the expression.

And now we can see how the third-person and first-person aspects of consciousness can be combined in a definition of consciousness. I suggest that we *define* an expression referring to some particular determination of consciousness—e.g., "pain"—in the following way: *it is that state which the subject usually notices to intervene between particular causal conditions and particular behavioral effects.* Here we have both aspects brought out in the two accounts we have examined. (1) We have the causal conditions and the behavioral effects, which provide the publicly observable setting. They allow us to specify the experience in public terms and to fix the meanings in an interpersonal linguistic scheme, so that the application of these terms to others is both intelligible and verifiable. (2) We have the private, inner experience, which is what actually is noticed to intervene in these circumstances. This gives us the *content* of the expression. Without it, we are in the position of Locke's "studious blind man"; he knew, as it were, the grammar or the use of color-words but he did not know the content or meanings of such words. The third-person account gives us, as it were, the addresses of states of consciousness in logical space, and the first-person account reminds us that we must look in at the address to see who lives there. We have a private, ostensive definition, but the directions for the ostensive definition are not private but public.

Analogies may mislead, but let me take that risk. Imagine that a particular length, say one meter, is defined as "whatever is the same length as a particular object, A, located in Paris."[9] That fixes the meaning of "one meter," and, in a way, we understand something by the expression when we hear it. But we do not as yet know how long a meter is and, therefore, do not fully understand the expression "one meter." When we are *shown* the object, A, or another object the same length, only then do we fully understand the expression. I am contending that expressions referring to experiences have the same feature.

Both third-person and first-person supporters have each seen part of the whole story. The third-person account explains how the meanings of these expressions are determined or fixed or given a location in the linguistic scheme, whereas the first-person account

[9] I am grateful to Mr. Michael Dunn for this example.

brings out the *content* of these expressions. There could be no content for psychological expressions unless the meanings were fixed; but without content there would be nothing to fix. Determinations of consciousness are not dispositions to respond which arise under certain conditions, as the behaviorist would have it, but they are by definition and hence necessarily the private, inner occurrences which usually go with those dispositions to respond.

Defenders of the third-person account might wish to raise some objections at this point to try to remove the private, inner, known-from-my-own-case element from the account of sensation-words I propose. The first is Wittgenstein's "beetle-in-the-box" objection. If we can fix the meanings of sensation-words by means of certain causal conditions (e.g., physical injury) and their effects (e.g., expression in behavior), then what point is there for the postulation of an intervening something which is the alleged content of the sensation-word? What conceivable role could it play in the language? Why should it not cancel out?[10]

Here one can only say that something does intervene, as the experience of mankind will testify. Remember Locke's story: The blind man did not get right what "scarlet" signifies, although he might have come to know everything about the term that a third-person account could teach him.

Experience shows that something does intervene between causal conditions and behavioral expression, but it must be admitted that experience does *not* show that this intervening something is what is meant by sensation-words. That is a philosophical thesis. Yet it is a plausible thesis, for (1) as we have seen, the meaning of sensation-words cannot be analyzed merely in terms of prior causes and subsequent effects, (2) it is precisely the occurrence of this intermediary which accounts for why the sighted person can learn the meanings of sensation-words and Locke's studious blind man does not, and (3) the intermediary is the only way of accounting for the epistemological asymmetry of first- and third-person reports.

The second objection comes from identity theorists (whose views will be discussed in more detail in Chapter 3). They would probably accept everything I have said so far about sensations, adding only that the intervening state between physical cause and be-

---

[10] "The thing in the box has no place in the language game at all; not even as a *something*: for the box might even be empty.—No, one can 'divide through' by the thing in the box: it cancels out, whatever it is." (*Philosophical Investigations*, sec. 293.)

havioral effect is a *brain state* (or, for some theorists, a state of the entire nervous system). Thus J. J. C. Smart takes a report of a sensation to be of the form "Something is going on in me which is like what [usually] goes on in me when . . ." where the "something" is not further specified by the reporter but neurological investigation will show it to be a brain state. Thus the referents of sensation-words are brain states. We are then left, essentially, with a third-person account.

My reply to this objection is as follows. If a person reports the having of some sensation, and, particularly, in line with Smart's suggestions, the having of something which is similar to what he has had before, he must have noticed some occurrence or some feature of some occurrence on the basis of which he makes his report. The sighted person notices something on the basis of which he recognizes that the afterimage is scarlet, in contrast to Locke's blind man who has not noticed any such feature. (Whether he could recognize something as scarlet immediately upon gaining his sight is the problem raised by Locke's friend Mr. Molyneux.) Now what one notices cannot, in the ordinary case, be said to be a neurological feature. The reporter is not in a position to say anything at all about the neurological features of the case, and it would be very odd to hold that he did notice some neurological feature if he was not in the slightest bit able to say anything at all about any neurological aspects of the situation.

A third objection to the account I have given of sensation-words is this: Surely there are other, equally plausible ways of accounting for the first-person element without postulating an inner, *private experience.* Consider the possibility of a person who can say what time it is without looking at a timepiece. Let us assume that he does not judge the time on the basis of some sensation but simply "guesses" what time it is and always gets it right. Could we not think of one's reporting of one's sensations in this way, and thus avoid postulating the inner experience? A person knows what sensation he has in the same way that our postulated time-knower knows that it is nine o'clock immediately and without observation, and yet without necessarily having a special, private nine o'clock feeling on the basis of which he judges that it is nine o'clock. On this account, sensation-reports are reports of what is public and observable by anyone, but it turns out that people can be trained to make such reports without resorting to observation of what is observable to anyone.

But there is an important difference between the case of the successful time-guesser and the person who reports having a sensation. The time of day is a fact establishable independently from the fact that our time-guesser guesses it correctly; he could lose the knack and have to go back to observing clocks. But it makes no sense to say that a person could lose the knack of describing his sensations without observing correctly and have to go back to observing his behavior to tell his sensations. Reporting a sensation is not reporting a public occurrence by some unusual, nonobservational method.

We can bring the case of the time-guesser closer to that of the person who reports having a sensation. Let us make it impossible for him to lose his knack. One way to do this is by making him, as it were, the Standard Clock, so that whatever time he says it is, becomes the time it is. But then his declarations are no longer reports which can be true or false; notice that he cannot even lie about the time. So we are still a long way from the case of sensations. A more interesting way of making it impossible for him to lose his knack is to construe his declaration as a report of what time *it feels to him to be*, e.g., that three-o'clock-in-the-morning feeling which characterizes Fitzgerald's "dark night of the soul." And now, of course, we no longer have an assertion of an independently establishable fact but the report of a sensation. So the analogy can no longer serve to help us *explain* sensation-words. Yet another case would be where the person simply reports his *inclination to guess* that it is three o'clock. And such a report would also be like the report of a sensation in some ways and unlike it in others.

Assuming that these objections have been met, a rather deep and dark difficulty remains. If we insist on distinguishing between the inner, private experience on the one hand, and its public causes and behavioral consequences on the other, it would seem that the relation between them is purely contingent, that the inner experience just happens to be preceded (usually) by public causes and effects; for, after all, as Hume pointed out, temporally distinct events are only contingently related. Yet do we not feel that there is more than just a contingent, causal connection between, say, experiencing severe pain and having a tendency to grimace, cry out, writhe, etc.? Could one really imagine that the world might have been quite different, composed solely of people who had not the slightest tendency to behave in these ways when experiencing severe pain? Could one really imagine that the world could have been made up of people who behaved in these ways when injured but never felt pain?

I will attempt, in a moment, to do justice to our feeling that there is more than a merely contingent relation between inner experience and outer antecedents and consequences. But before I do so, let me emphasize one point I have already argued for. There is no logical connection between being in pain and its (usual) causal antecedents and consequences. Neither one is logically necessary nor sufficient for the other; each could occur without the other.

However, on the account I have given, we would not have the concepts we do unless they did usually go together. For the concepts we have, if I am right, are ones in which a private ostensive definition is given by public instructions—and if the inner experience did not accompany the outer conditions, then no private ostensive definition would occur, and thus our concept would be empty. That our concepts have content results from a contingent fact. And that our concepts have content entails that this contingent fact obtains. So when we puzzle over how a world could have been composed of people who *felt* pain but never *expressed* it or *behaved* as if in pain but never *felt* pain, then the source of our puzzlement is the fact that in such a world our concept of pain would have no application. And if it had no application, it could not be said either that such people felt pain or that they did not feel pain; so there could not be such a world. But that does not show that there is a necessary connection between pain and its causal surroundings. It simply shows that a world in which the concept of pain does have application could not be such a world. Nothing here said rules out that there could be a tribe somewhere for whose members these causal conditions did not obtain. But they could not learn our concept of pain.

THE SUBJECT

OF CONSCIOUSNESS

3

It would seem to be an undeniable fact that consciousness does exist and that any account of the world will have to give some place to it. But what place? What is the relation of consciousness to whatever else does exist? In particular, what is the relation of consciousness to the organic and inorganic matter that makes up so great a part of the world? And, more particularly, what is the relation of consciousness to those organic systems we know as human bodies? This is the question which will occupy us in the next two chapters.

We can begin our inquiry by asking what is the subject of consciousness, in other words, *what* is conscious when consciousness exists? Well, what sorts of things have consciousness? One pretty indisputable case is that of men or human beings. But what is a man or human being? Is he just a particular kind of matter formed in a particular way? Or is there more to the story, and if so what more? If a man is *more* than a particularly formed kind of matter, then is it some part of that *more* which is the subject of consciousness?-

To make the discussion manageable, let us confine ourselves to that form of consciousness which consists in having what I shall call mental events: those particular occasions which consist in the having of some thought, the feeling of some sensation, the imaging of some mental picture, the entertaining of some wish, etc. Our problem, then, will be to determine *what* it is that has the thought, feels the sensation, images the mental picture, entertains the wish, etc.

The various theories concerning *what* has the mental events fall into three basic categories. (1) There is the view that they happen to purely *nonmaterial* things. Proponents of such a view usually admit the existence of purely *material* things in addition to these purely nonmaterial things; hence they are called dualists. (2) There is the view that they happen to purely *material* things; we shall call this materialism. And (3) there is the view that they happen to things which are neither purely material nor purely nonmaterial; we shall call this the person theory. Each shall be considered and evaluated in turn.

Dualism   The most systematic dualistic theory is that which was presented by the French philosopher Descartes. He held that the subject of consciousness is the *mind* and that the mind is a thing or entity separate and distinct from the body. The body is a thing or entity whose essence (defining characteristic) is occupying space, i.e., having shape, size, and location in space; and it is in no sense conscious. The mind, on the other hand, is completely different in its nature. It is utterly nonspatial, having neither shape, size, nor location. Its essence (defining characteristic) is simply having consciousness, that is, thoughts, feelings, memories, perceptions, desires, emotions, etc.

Descartes held that since the mind and the body are separate entities, each can exist without the other. It is obvious and undeniable that Descartes is at least correct in holding that *some* bodies— e.g., stones and lakes—do indeed exist without minds. Descartes himself believed that animals (other than man) were also examples of bodies without minds. Some people might disagree with him there, and there would be even more disagreement with his thesis that minds could exist without bodies. Descartes believed that minds were immortal, that they continue to exist as disembodied minds after the body has perished in death.

There is an important gap in Descartes' account, a gap which can be noted in the summary just given. From the fact that the essence of the mind is one thing, having consciousness, and the essence of the body is another, occupying space, it does not follow that the mind and the body are *two separate entities*. What is to rule out the possibility that one and the same thing can have *both* these properties, be *both* a thinking thing and at the very same time an extended thing? The essence, that is, the defining characteristic, of being a husband is being a married man and the essence of being a parent is having offspring, but one and the same person can be both a husband *and* a parent (and, obviously, can be one without being the other). This gap in Descartes' reasoning was first pointed out by Spinoza, who had been a follower of Descartes. Spinoza realized that "although two attributes may be conceived as really distinct," and here he has in mind thinking and extension, "we cannot nevertheless thence conclude that they constitute two beings or two different substances." [1] Then, breaking decisively with Descartes, Spinoza went on to maintain that in the case of human beings (and, as a matter of fact, for Spinoza, in everything else as well), both thinking *and* space-occupancy were characteristics of one and the same thing. This view shall be discussed later under the heading of double aspect theory.

Nevertheless, Descartes held that one and the same thing could not be both a space-occupier and a thinking thing. He seems to have thought that these characteristics were simply so different in their natures that one and the same thing *could* not have both. Thus he cites the fact that extended things are divisible, whereas thinking things are not divisible (see his sixth *Meditation*). But this is a very weak line of argument. Since thinking and occupying space are different characteristics, there will naturally be differences between them. Extended things will necessarily be divisible (I take it Descartes is here thinking of *spatially* dividing something), and things which are nonextended, say disembodied minds, will not be so divisible. But that is just to say that we have different characteristics here. A thing which thinks would be divisible if it were at the same time an extended thing. So pointing out differences between extension and thinking does not show us that things which have the one characteristic cannot have the other. Perhaps Descartes had in mind the point that extension and thinking are *so very* different, so basically different. Of course one object could be both red and round, he might say, but could one object be both red and thinking? Here again, however, the line of argument is weak. Being red and being valuable and being holy are *very* different sorts of properties, yet one and the same object, say a particular jewel, might be all three. So we still do not have a very good reason for thinking that thinking things could not be extended and vice versa.

Even if the dualist fails to give us a reason for holding that thinking things and extended things are *different* entities, still such a view might be correct. And we have not yet seen any reason for thinking it is *not* correct. So let us, for the moment, grant the dualist his claim that they are different entities. If we do so, the question arises how these two different entities are related to each other, if at all.

[1] *Ethics*, Part I, Prop. X, note.

Here we find ourselves faced with what is traditionally known in philosophy as the mind-body problem.

The traditional mind-body problem   A full discussion of the mind-body problem will be reserved for Chapter 4. But in order to get a better grasp of dualism we will here take a brief look at the various theories that have been proposed. Descartes himself believed that sometimes the mind could causally affect the body and sometimes the body could causally affect the mind; this view is called interactionism. An example of the former would be a case in which, after deliberation, I decide (a mental event) to press the button and then my hand reaches out to press it (a bodily event); an example of the latter would be a case in which the moving hand (a bodily event) comes in contact with the button, causing in me a feeling of fear (a mental event) at what will happen if I do press the button.

Interactionism is not the only dualistic theory of the relation between mind and body. Some philosophers have held that there is only *one-way* causality, from body to mind; this view is known as epiphenomenalism. The epiphenomenalist accepts one half of the interactionist contention, that part which holds that bodily events can cause mental events. But he denies the other half; he denies that mental events can ever cause bodily events. Whatever happens in the mind is merely a by-product of bodily activity (most plausibly, brain activity). No important philosopher has ever held what we might call reverse epiphenomenalism, namely that bodily events are *always* merely effects of mental activity. The religion of Christian Science comes somewhat close to this view, holding that bodily events, particularly those concerning health and disease, are results of mental activity. Many Christian Scientists would go so far as to maintain that *all* bodily events, for example the activity in our sense organs during perception, are caused solely by mental activity. This is the view of the eighteenth century Irish philosopher George Berkeley, that anything that ever happens at all happens only in the mind. Berkeley's view is no longer dualism; he holds that only minds exist and that matter and in particular bodies do not exist at all, except in the mind.

Finally, there is the dualist theory known as parallelism. The parallelist admits the close connection of events in the mind and events in the body, but does not wish to say that the connection is a causal one, for he holds that the mind and the body are too utterly different to be able to interact causally with each other. So the parallelist holds that the mind and the body are like two clocks, each with its own mechanism and with no causal connection between them, yet always in phase keeping the same time.

Dualist theories are not very much in favor these days. There are two main sources of discontent with them. (1) Many philosophers have grave doubts that the notion of the mind as a thing or entity can be rendered intelligible. (2) Even if it could be made intelligible, the view of the world which results seems to many unnecessarily complex. We will discuss these two sources of discontent in order.

(1) Dualists tell us that in addition to the familiar objects of everyday life, tables, rocks, hair, trees, clouds, air, in short material things, there also exist things of a quite different kind—minds. These minds are real things, real objects, real entities, but they are fundamentally different sorts of things from material things. Well then, what is a mind? Is it a peculiar kind of stuff, immaterial matter, insubstantial substance, bodiless body? It is supposed to have no extension, that is, no shape, size, or capacity to occupy space; it is not visible to the eye, tangible to the touch, nor is it visible under any microscope however powerful, tangible to the most delicate of probing instruments. Perhaps the mind is like a gravitational, magnetic, or electrical field? But it cannot be, for on the dualist's hypothesis the mind is in no way physical; if it were like them, or like physical energy of some sort, then it would be a *physical* phenomenon and we would no longer be dualists. Yet if it is in no way like such things, in what sense is the mind a thing at all? What meaning can we give to the notion of the mind as an existent thing?

The problem comes out in two particular ways, in the problem of identification and the problem of individuation. The former problem concerns how we can tell when we are in the presence of some other mind A rather than B or even in the presence of any other mind at all. Since, on the dualist account, another mind is not detectable by any observations we could make, it is impossible that we should have any reason to think we could ever identify another mind as mind A or B. So we could never justifiably believe we were, for example, talking to someone. And a concept of a mind which made it impossible justifiably to apply that concept to any other thing would be utterly useless, even if intelligible.

The problem of individuation concerns what makes two minds distinct, assuming there could be two distinct minds. One answer might be that they have different mental histories, each having had different mental events at certain times. But it seems perfectly intelligible to suppose that at some time we might have two distinct minds with exactly the same history of mental events (each might have grown up in exactly the same way). And, if this supposition of two exactly similar minds is intelligible, then what would make them two distinct minds rather than one and the same mind? The dualist does not seem to have an answer. He must say they are distinct, and yet he cannot say how or in what respect they differ. Does that make any sense?

(2) Even if we were able to give some *meaning* to the claim that minds exist, many contemporary philosophers would reject the claim that in fact minds do exist. They would make the remark attributed to the French astronomer Laplace in reply to Napoleon's question about the role of God in the system: said Laplace, "Sire, I have no need of that hypothesis." Thus many philosophers would argue that everything that happens in the world can be explained without using the notion of minds, strictly on the basis of physical phenomena and physical laws.

The view that minds do not exist at all and that only the physical exists is called materialism. We shall now turn to this view.

Materialism Materialism is one of the very oldest theories. It was a familiar doctrine to the ancient Greeks of the fourth and fifth centuries B.C. The spokesman for this view, Democritus, held that nothing exists but material atoms and the void and that everything in the world is nothing but the interactions of these atoms as they move through the void. Even the most complex behavior of human beings can be resolved into interactions between the atoms. A modern materialist would allow a more complicated picture than "atoms and the void." He would bring in subatomic particles and antiparticles, electromagnetic waves, a relativized view of "the void," various kinds of forces and energies, and the rest of the conceptual apparatus of contemporary physics. But he would still hold that nothing exists but such physical phenomena; if such terms as "thought," "feeling," "wish," etc., have any meaning at all, they must refer in the last analysis to physical phenomena. So-called mental events are really nothing but physical events occurring to physical objects.

We should, at the outset, distinguish materialism as characerized here from another doctrine which has already been mentioned, epiphenomenalism (see page 37, above). The latter is a dualistic theory which allows that the mind is separate and distinct from the body but also insists that the mind is utterly dependent causally upon the body, that everything which happens in the mind is a result of events in the body, and that the mind is utterly power-less to affect the body in any way. Such a view is often called ma-terialistic, since it places the highest *importance* on the material side of things. It is in this sense that Karl Marx was materialistic, for he held that "conceiving, thinking, the mental intercourse of men, appear at [the earliest] stage as the direct efflux of their ma-terial behavior." [2] Notice that Marx is not saying men's conceiving, thinking, and mental intercourse *are nothing but* their material be-havior. That would be materialism as here characterized. He is say-ing that they are the "efflux," i.e., a *separate, nonmaterial* outflow which originates and derives from material behavior. Such a view is not materialistic in our sense.

The materialist holds that nothing but the physical exists—matter, energy, and the void. But then what *are* thoughts, feelings, wishes, and the other so-called mental phenomena? Here four differ-ent answers have been seriously proposed. The most radical view, supported by very few, is that such terms have *no real meaning at all* and should be dropped from the language. They represent an ac-cretion to our language which was conceived in ignorance and super-stition, nurtured by the vested interests of religion and the black arts, and condoned by human lethargy. On this view, mentalistic terms should be allowed to suffer the fate of the language of witch-craft and demonic possession. Let us call this the unintelligibility thesis.

The unintelligibility thesis has not gained much support among contemporary philosophers. In the first place, it is clear why notions of witchcraft and demonic possession died out—it has been shown pretty conclusively by science that no such phenomena in fact exist. There might have been witches, and, in that case, there could have been a science which studied them and the ways in which they achieved their effects; but the evidence indicates that there are no such things. But this is hardly the case with mentalistic terms. What kind of discoveries could show that in fact there are no thoughts, feelings, wishes, and the like? On the contrary, is it not as plain as anything can be that there are such things? And, secondly, we could not dispense with mentalistic terms, even if our theories told us it was most desirable to do so, nor does it seem likely we will be able to do for the foreseeable future. This is because we often want to tell our thoughts, describe our feelings, express our wishes, and there is no other way available of doing so than saying I just had the

[2] Karl Marx and Friedrich Engels, *The German Ideology* (New York: Inter-national Publishers, 1947), p. 14.

thought . . . , I feel . . . , I wish . . . . To abandon such expressions would be to impoverish our language to the point of bankruptcy.

Another materialistic reply to the question "What are thoughts, feelings, wishes, and the like?" is called the avowal theory. This theory allows that sentences like "I feel bored" have meaning all right, but are not used to make *statements*, are not used to describe or report or assert anything. They are simply bits of behavior, the effects of certain inner (physical) conditions. If I yawn, twiddle my thumbs, or say "Ho hum," I am not describing, reporting, or asserting anything; I am not making a statement which is either true or false. The avowal theory takes "I feel bored" to be a (learned) bit of behavior, like "Ho hum," which results from certain inner (physical) conditions, and not a statement, description, report, or assertion at all. And the same would go for utterances of the form "I just had the thought that . . . ," "I wish that . . . ," and the like.

It cannot be denied that there is some truth in the avowal theory. Certainly such utterances are sometimes used in this way, as expressions of inner states—"I feel bored" is sometimes uttered in the way that "God, I'm bored!" or even "Oh God, what boredom!" is uttered, and it is clear at least in the latter case that no statement, description, report, or assertion is being made. Yet the avowal theory falls down in two important respects. First, it is utterly implausible when applied to third-person statements, e.g., "He is bored." In no way can such a remark be taken as the expression of an inner state. Second, even in their first-person use, such utterances are often used merely to report or describe. If someone asks me why I keep looking at my watch, I may say "Because I am bored," making a report which explains my behavior. Furthermore, I can use such utterances to make *false* statements, as when I am lying. "Ho hum" cannot be used to explain anything or to lie about anything. So the avowal theory will not do.

Another materialistic account is to allow that expressions referring to thoughts, feelings, wishes, and the like have meaning, but to insist that their meanings can be expressed in purely physicalistic terms. What physicalistic terms? The most plausible candidate is the set of terms which refer to physical *behavior*. This account, known as behaviorism, was discussed in Chapter 2 (see pages 15-21, above).

This behavioristic version of materialism has had a strong appeal for philosophers over the years. In contrast with the unintelligibility thesis, it allows sentences containing mentalistic terms to have meaning, and, in contrast with the avowal theory, it allows them to be either true or false in the situations in which they are used. And by using the concept of *disposition to behave*, it allows such sentences to be true even where the person is not at that moment behaving in any particular fashion. Yet by tying the meaning to *behavior* the theory allows sentences with mentalistic terms to be testable by observation in an open and public way. To determine whether someone has a headache we only have to see if, under suitable conditions, he behaves in the appropriate ways.

This view, however, is open to a fundamental objection, as we have already seen. No matter what sort of behavior or behavioral dispositions we imagine as allegedly constituting a particular mental event, we can always imagine just that behavior or those dispositions *without* that mental event. We can imagine that behavior as coming from some *other* cause, or even as inexplicably *spontaneous*. Therefore behavior and behavioral dispositions do not furnish an exhaustive analysis of these mentalistic terms. There is something left out by such accounts.

The last version of materialism we shall consider, and currently the most seriously discussed, is known as the identity theory. It is the theory that thoughts, feelings, wishes, and the rest of so-called mental phenomena are identical with, one and the same thing as, states and processes of the *body* (and, perhaps, more specifically, states and processes of the nervous system, or even of the brain alone). Thus the having of a thought is identical with having such and such bodily cells in such and such states, other cells in other states.

In one respect the identity theory and behaviorism are very much alike. This comes out when we ask ourselves what the "dispositions" of the behaviorist are. If an object has a "disposition," then *it is in a particular state* such that when certain things happen to it, other things will happen to it. Thus if an object is brittle, it is in a particular state such that when subject to a sudden force it will shatter. And similarly dispositions of a body to behave in particular ways are *states of that body*. So it is fair to say that both identity theorists and behaviorists identify the mental with *bodily states*. But one important way in which they differ concerns how those states are to be defined or characterized. As we have seen, behaviorists wish to define those states in terms of what changes they result in when certain specifiable conditions obtain. Identity theorists wish to define them in terms of identifiable structures of the body, ongoing processes and states of the bodily organs, and, in the last analysis, the very cells which go to make up those organs.

There is another important respect in which the identity theory differs from behaviorism. The behaviorist offered his notion of dispositions to behave in certain ways as an analysis of the very meaning of mentalistic terms. But the identity theorist grants that it is wildly implausible to claim that what I *mean* when I say, for example, that I just had a particular thought is that certain events were going on in my nervous system. For I have no idea what those events are, nor does even the most advanced neurophysiologist at the present time, and yet I know what I mean when I say I just had a particular thought. So, since I know what I mean by those words, I cannot mean by them something I know nothing about (viz., unknown events in my nervous system). Hence the identity theory is not intended to be an analysis of the *meanings* of mentalistic terms as behaviorism purports to be. What, then, is the theory that mental phenomena are "identical" with the body intended to be?

The sense of "identity" relevant here is that in which we say, for example, that the morning star is "identical" with the evening star. It is not that the expression "morning star" means the same as the expression "evening star"; on the contrary, these expressions mean something different. But the object referred to by the two expressions is one and the same; there is just one heavenly body, namely, Venus, which when seen in the morning is called the morning star and when seen in the evening is called the evening star. The morning star is identical with the evening star; they are one and the same object.

Of course, the identity of the mental with the physical is not exactly of this sort, since it is held to be simultaneous identity rather than the identity of a thing at one time with the same thing at a later time. To take a closer example, one can say that lightning is a particularly massive electrical discharge from one cloud to another or to the earth. Not that the word "lightning" *means* "a particularly massive electrical discharge . . . "; when Benjamin Franklin discovered that lightning was electrical, he did not make a discovery about the meaning of words. Nor when it was discovered that water was H_2O was a discovery made about the meanings of words; yet water is identical with H_2O.

In a similar fashion, the identity theorist can hold that thoughts, feelings, wishes, and the like are identical with physical states. Not "identical" in the sense that mentalistic terms are synonymous in meaning with physicalistic terms but "identical" in the sense that the actual events picked out by mentalistic terms are one and the same events as those picked out by physicalistic terms.

It is important to note that the identity theory does not have a chance of being true unless a particular sort of correspondence obtains between mental events and physical events, namely, that whenever a mental event occurs, a physical event of a particular sort (or at least one of a number of particular sorts) occurs, and vice versa. If it turned out to be the case that when a particular mental event occurred it seemed a matter of chance what physical events occurred or even whether any physical event at all occurred, or vice versa, then the identity theory would not be true. So far as our state of knowledge at the present time is concerned, it is still too early to say what the empirical facts are, although it must be said that many scientists do believe that there exists the kind of correspondences needed by identity theorists. But even if these correspondences turn out to exist, that does not mean that the identity theory will be true. For identity theorists do not hold merely that mental and physical events are correlated in a particular way but that they are one and the same events, i.e., not like lightning and thunder (which are correlated in lawful ways but not identical) but like lightning and electrical discharges (which always go together because they are one and the same).

What are the advantages of the identity theory? As a form of materialism, it does not have to cope with a world which has in it both mental phenomena and physical phenomena, and it does not have to ponder how they might be related. There exist only the physical phenomena, although there do exist two different ways of talking about such phenomena: physicalistic terminology and, in at least some situations, mentalistic terminology. We have here a dualism of language, but not a dualism of entities, events, or properties.

Some difficulties in the identity theory

But we do have merely a dualism of languages and no other sort of dualism? In the case of Venus, we do indeed have only one object, but the expression "morning star" picks out one phase of that object's history, where it is in the mornings, and the expression "evening star" picks out another phase of that object's history, where it is in the evenings. If that object did not have these two distinct aspects, it would not have been a *discovery* that the morning star and the evening star were indeed one and the same body, and, further, there would be no point to the different ways of referring to it.

Now it would be admitted by identity theorists that physicalistic and mentalistic terms do not refer to different phases in the history of one and the same object. What sort of identity is intended?

Let us turn to an allegedly closer analogy, that of the identity of lightning and a particular sort of electrical phenomenon. Yet here again we have two distinguishable aspects, the appearance to the naked eye on the one hand and the physical composition on the other. And this is also not the kind of identity which is plausible for mental and physical events. The appearance *to the naked eye* of a neurological event is utterly different from the experience of having a thought or a pain.

It is sometimes suggested that the physical aspect results from looking at a particular event "from the outside," whereas the mental results from looking at the same event "from the inside." When the brain surgeon observes my brain he is looking at it from the outside, whereas when I experience a mental event I am "looking" at my brain "from the inside."

Such an account gives us only a misleading analogy, rather than an accurate characterization of the relationship between the mental and the physical. The analogy suggests the difference between a man who knows his own house from the inside, in that he is free to move about within, seeing objects from different perspectives, touching them, etc., but can never get outside to see how it looks from there, and a man who cannot get inside and therefore knows only the outside appearance of the house, and perhaps what he can glimpse through the windows. But what does this have to do with the brain? Am I free to roam about inside my brain, observing what the brain surgeon may never see? Is not the "inner" aspect of my brain far more accessible to the brain surgeon than to me? He has the X rays, probes, electrodes, scalpels, and scissors for getting at the inside of my brain. If it is replied that this is only an analogy, not to be taken literally, then the question still remains how the mental and the physical are related.

Usually identity theorists at this point flee to even vaguer accounts of the relationship. They talk of different "levels of analysis," or of different "perspectives," or of different "conceptual schemes," or of different "language games." The point of such suggestions is that the difference between the mental and the physical is not a basic, fundamental, or intrinsic one, but rather a difference which is merely relative to different human purposes or standpoints. The difference is supposed to exist not in the thing itself but in the eye of the beholder.

But these are only hints. They do not tell us in precise and literal terms how the mental and the physical differ and are related. They only try to assure us that the difference does not matter to the real nature of things. But until we are given a theory to consider, we cannot accept the identity theorists' assurance that some theory will do only he does not know what it is.

One of the leading identity theorists, J. J. C. Smart, holds that mentalistic discourse is simply a vaguer, more indefinite way of talking about what could be talked about more precisely by using physiological terms. If I report a red afterimage, I mean (roughly) that something is going on which is like what goes on when I really see a red patch. I do not actually *mean* that a particular sort of brain process is occurring, but when I say something is going on I refer (very vaguely, to be sure) to just that brain process. Thus the thing referred to in my report of an afterimage is a brain process. Hence there is no need to bring in any nonphysical features. Thus even the taint of dualism is avoided.

Does this ingenious attempt to evade dualistic implications stand up under philosophical scrutiny? I am inclined to think it will not. Let us return to the man reporting the red afterimage. He was aware of the occurrence of something or other, of some feature or other. Now it seems to me obvious that he was not necessarily aware of the state of his brain at that time (I doubt that most of us are ever aware of the state of our brain) nor, in general, necessarily aware of any physical features of his body at that time. He might, of course, have been incidentally aware of some physical feature but not insofar as he was aware of the red afterimage as such. Yet he was definitely aware of something, or else how could he have made that report? So he must have been aware of some nonphysical feature. That is the only way of explaining how he was aware of anything at all.

Of course, the thing that our reporter of the afterimage was aware of might well have had further features which he was *not* aware of, particularly, in this connection, physical features. I may be aware of certain features of an object without being aware of others. So it is not ruled out that the event our reporter is aware of might be an event with predominantly physical features—he just does not notice those. But he must be aware of some of its features, or else it would not be proper to say he was aware of *that* event. And if he is not aware of any physical features, he must be aware of something else. And that shows that we cannot get rid of those nonphysical features in the way that Smart suggests.

One would not wish to be dogmatic in saying that identity theorists will never work out this part of their theory. Much work is being done on this problem at the present time, for it arises in other areas of philosophy as well as in the philosophy of mind. In particular philosophers of science are concerned with the problem. We saw that the identity theory used such analogies as the identity of lightning with electrical phenomena and the identity of water with molecules consisting of hydrogen and oxygen. But the question to be raised is what kind of identity we are dealing with in such cases. Do we have mere duality of terms in these cases, duality of features, properties, or aspects, or even duality of substances? Very similar issues arise. So it is quite possible that further work on this problem of identity will be useful in clarifying the identity theory of the mental and the physical. But at the present the matter is by no means as clear as it should be.

Even if the identity theorist could clarify the sense of "identity" to be used in his theory, he would still face two other problems. These concern coexistence in time and space. Coexistence in time and space are conditions that must be met if there is to be identity. That is to say, for two apparently different things to turn out to be one and the same, they must exist at the same time and in the same location. If we could show that Mr. A existed at a time when Mr. B did not, or that Mr. A existed in a place where Mr. B did not, then this would show that Mr. A and Mr. B were different men. It is by virtue of these facts about identity that an alibi can exonerate a suspect: if Mr. A was not in Chicago at the time, then he could not be one and the same with the man who stole the diamonds in Chicago.

So if mental events are to be identical with physical events, then they must fulfill the conditions of coexistence in time and space. The question is, Do they?

So far as coexistence in time is concerned, very little is known. The most relevant work consists in direct stimulation of an exposed part of the brain during surgery. Since only a local anesthetic is necessary in many such cases the patient may well be fully conscious. Then, as the surgeon stimulates different parts of his brain, the patient may report the occurrence of mental events—memories, thoughts, sensations. Do the physical events in the brain and the mental events occur at precisely the same time? It is impossible to say. All that would be required is a very small time gap to prove that the physical events were not identical with the mental events. But it is very difficult to see how the existence of so small a time gap could be established. And even if it were, what would it prove? Only that the mental event was not identical with just that physical event; it would not prove it was nonidentical with any physical event. So it could well be that coexistence in time is present or is not. I do not think that we shall get much decisive information from empirical work of the sort here described. The identity theorist, then, does not have to fear refutation from this quarter, at least not for a long time.

How about coexistence in space? Do mental events occur in the same place the corresponding physical events occur? This is also a very difficult question to answer, for two reasons. First our present ignorance of neurophysiology, especially concerning the brain and how it functions, allows us to say very little about the location of the relevant physical events. This much does seem likely: they are located in the brain. Much more than that we do not at present know, although as the time passes, we should learn much more. The second reason for our difficulty in telling if there is coexistence in space has to do with the location of mental events. Where do thoughts, feelings, and wishes occur? Do they occur in the brain? Suppose you suddenly have the thought that it is almost suppertime; where does that occur? The most sensible answer would be that it occurs wherever you are when you have that thought. If you are in the library when you have that thought, then the thought occurs in the library. But it would be utterly unnatural to ask where inside your body the thought occurred; in your foot, or your liver, or your heart, or your head? It is not that any one of these places is more likely than another. They are all wrong. Not because thoughts occur somewhere *else* within your body than your foot, liver, heart, or head—but because it *makes no sense at all* to locate the occurrence of a thought at some place within your body. We would not understand someone who pointed to a place in his body and claimed that it was *there* that his entertaining of a thought was located. Certainly, if one *looked* at that place, one would not *see* anything resembling a thought. If it were replied to this that pains can be located in the body without being seen there, then it should be pointed out that one *feels* the pain there but one hardly feels a thought in the body.

The fact that it makes no sense at all to speak of mental events as occurring at some point within the body has the result that the identity theory cannot be true. This is because the corresponding physical events do occur at some point within the body, and if those physical events are identical with mental events, then those mental events must occur at the same point within the body. But those mental events do not occur at any point within the body, because any statement to the effect that they occurred here, or there, would be senseless. Hence the mental events cannot meet the condition of coexistence in space, and therefore cannot be identical with physical events.

Our inability to give the location within the body of mental events is different from our inability to give the location of the corresponding physical events within the body. In the latter case, it is that we do not know enough about the body, particularly the brain. Some day, presumably, we will know enough to pin down pretty exactly the location of the relevant physical events. But in the case of mental events it is not simply that at present we are ignorant but that someday we may well know. What would it be like to discover the location of a thought in the brain? What kind of information would we need to be able to say that the thought occurred exactly *here*? If by X rays or some other means we were able to see every event which occurred in the brain, we would never get a glimpse of a thought. If, to resort to fantasy, we could so enlarge a brain or so shrink ourselves that we could wander freely through the brain, we would still never observe a thought. All we could ever observe in the brain would be the *physical* events which occur in it. If mental events had location in the brain, there should be some means of detecting them there. But of course there is none. The very idea of it is senseless.

Some identity theorists believe this objection can be met. One approach is to reply that this objection begs the question: if the identity theory is true, and mental events are identical with brain events, then, paradoxical as it may sound, mental events do indeed have location, and are located precisely where the physical events are located. Another approach is to reply that the relevant physical events should be construed as events which happen to the body as a whole, and therefore occur where the body as a whole is located; then it is not so paradoxical to give location to the mental events, for they would be located where the body is located but would not be located in any particular part of the body.

We have carried our discussion of the identity theory to the very frontier of present philosophical thinking. We can only leave it to the reader to decide how well it can meet the objections which are raised to it.

There is a mixed theory which is relevant at this point. A person might hold that, although mental and physical events are different sorts of events and in no sense identical, nevertheless the subjects to which they both occur are *material* objects. Thus we have a theory which preserves materialism so far as the *subject* of these events is concerned, but represents an important departure from materialism in accepting a dualism of *events*, the existence of nonmaterial events which happen to material objects in addition to the material events which happen to them.

It would be a mere verbal evasion at this point to argue that so-called mental events are really physical, in this mixed theory, since they occur to physical objects. What would have to be faced is the fact that thoughts, feelings, wishes, and the like are happenings of a quite different sort from the changes in size, shape, location, charge, spin, energy level, etc., which are countenanced in present physical theory. And if we did find even more occult and unfamiliar sorts of physical events, we would still have to face the question whether these events are identical with thoughts, feelings, etc. And any attempt to argue for identity would face all the problems we have already observed to arise for the identity theory.

If we were to accept a dualism of events, then to that extent we would be abandoning materialism. We would be admitting that what exists is not merely or purely or wholly material. Objects would have a nonmaterial dimension; they would be subject to nonmaterial happenings and nonmaterial states. To that extent, objects would not be merely material in nature. On the other hand, there would be no merely or purely or wholly nonmaterial objects which were subjects of mental events either. So we would not be back in a full-fledged dualism either. The kind of theory we would have is a neutralist theory: what at the beginning of this chapter we called the person theory. It is time we turned to a full examination of that theory.

A double aspect account   We have considered the view that mental events happen to purely immaterial substances and the view that so-called mental events are physical events which happen to purely material substances. We have seen both advantages and disadvantages in each of these main lines of approach. Dualism does justice to what we take to be the wide gulf between the conscious, on the one hand, and matter on the other, but at the expense of introducing the very mysterious notion of the purely thinking substance. Materialism dispenses with such a notion, but at the expense of obliterating what we take to be an ineradicable gulf between the conscious and matter. We will shortly look at a recent attempt to find a compromise between these two theories. We will call it the person theory. It is the view that mental events happen neither to purely immaterial substances nor to purely material substances, but to some thing which is *neither immaterial nor material*; let us call them persons.

Mental events happen to *persons,* and persons are subject to *both* mental *and* material happenings.

The historical ancestor of the person theorist is Spinoza, the Dutch philosopher of the seventeenth century. Confronted on the one side by the English materialist Hobbes and on the other side by the French dualist Descartes, Spinoza said, in effect, a plague on both your houses. The mental and the physical are both of them simply aspects of something which in itself is neither mental nor physical. A man can equally well be considered as an extended, physical thing or as a thinking thing, although each of these characterizations only brings out one aspect of the man. The analogy has been proposed of an undulating line which at a given moment may be concave from one point of view and convex from the other. The line itself is not completely described by either term, but only by the use of both terms. Yet it is not that there are two different things, one concave and the other convex. There is only one thing which is, from one point of view, concave and, from another point of view, convex. So with man. He is both a thinking thing and an extended, physical thing—not that he is two things but rather that he is one thing with these two aspects. Such a view is traditionally known as a double aspect view. It is like some versions of the identity theory, but, at least in Spinoza's case, differs with respect to the conception of the thing that has the two aspects. For Spinoza what has the two aspects is not material (nor is it mental either), whereas for the identity theory as we have discussed it what has the two aspects is material.

Although we cannot examine the details of Spinoza's theory, we might note that Spinoza believed *everything* which existed had these two aspects. This view is called panpsychism. It is the view that consciousness occurs wherever anything exists and thus that every tree, rock, cloud, and even every atom is conscious to some degree. To be sure, Spinoza did not believe that all things had so fully developed a consciousness as man has; presumably a rock's mind is so crude and inferior that it is only barely conscious at all. Still, for Spinoza, it is conscious to some degree.

For a double aspect theory, there are two issues of crucial importance—what is the nature of the underlying stuff which has the aspects, and what exactly are "aspects"? Unfortunately in Spinoza's theory both of these are left in deep obscurity. Each man, and, in fact, everything else that exists, is just a particular instance or specimen of what Spinoza calls "Substance" and also calls "God" or "Nature." But it is very difficult to understand what this stuff is. An indication of the difficulty is that since Spinoza's time there has been an unending controversy whether Spinoza was an atheist or what one commentator called "a God-intoxicated man." If an issue so general as that cannot be settled, then it is unlikely that we can hope for much clarification about the nature of this underlying stuff. The second question, What is an "aspect"?, is equally important to answer, for we do not know what it means to say that the mental and the physical are "aspects" of the same thing until we know what an "aspect" is. Again, Spinoza is not of much help. In his theory, the mental and the physical are both basic attributes of the underlying stuff but he never says how they are related or, indeed, how one and the same thing could have such *different* attributes. As we saw in our discussion of the identity theory (see p. 45), it is very difficult to explain with any precision in what sense the mental and the physical are "aspects." The suggestion, by analogy with perception, is that they are different appearances of the thing, the thing as seen from different points of view, but when we try to replace the analogy with a literal characterization, we find ourselves unable to say very much.

The person theory   In recent philosophy, a modified version of the double aspect theory which we will call the person theory has been presented by P. F. Strawson.[3] It is the view that the mental and the physical are both of them attributes of *persons*; the person is the underlying entity which has both mental and physical attributes. Thus we could say of the *person* that he is six feet tall, weighs one hundred and seventy-five pounds, is moving at the rate of three miles an hour (all physical attributes), and we could also say of the very same entity, that person, that he is now thinking about a paper he is writing, feels a pang of anxiety about that paper, and then wishes it were already over and done with (all mental attributes). We have here neither attributions to two different subjects, a mind and a body (dualism), nor attributions to a body (materialism), but attributions to a person. We may say that the person has a mind and a body, but all that means is that both mental and physical attributes are applicable to him.

Why does Strawson reject materialism and hold that mental states must be attributed to a *person* rather than to a body? His argument is very difficult to grasp but it appears to be as follows.[4] Unless we are to accept the unintelligibility thesis or the avowal theory (see pp. 40-41, above)—theories which Strawson rejects as too

[3] P. F. Strawson, *Individuals* (London: Methuen & Co., Ltd., 1959), Chapter 3.
[4] *Ibid.*, pp. 95-98.

paradoxical to consider—we must admit that we often do ascribe states of consciousness to things; e.g., we say of some particular subject that the subject had a headache. Now Strawson wishes to argue that the notion of attributing a state of consciousness to a subject cannot be analyzed as the notion of attributing a state of consciousness to a body. Consider the epiphenomenalist, who claims that to say "Subject A has a headache" is synonymous with saying "Body *a* is producing a headache." Now the epiphenomenalist would grant that this contention—that all of subject A's headaches are produced by body *a*—is *controversial*, and that some argumentation is needed. But what exactly is the contention? It is not that *all* headaches are produced by body *a*. That is obviously false. Only subject A's headaches are produced by body *a*. But if "Subject A has a headache" is synonymous with "Body *a* is producing a headache," then to say "All subject A's headaches are produced by body *a*" is simply to say "All the headaches produced by body *a* are produced by body *a*." And that is a claim about which controversy would be impossible, since it is an utter tautology. Exactly the same reasoning would be directed by Strawson against the kind of materialism which holds that "Subject A has a headache" means "Body *a* has a headache."

Strawson's point, if we are interpreting him properly, is that in order for materialists and epiphenomenalists even to formulate their claim, they must have a concept of a subject of mental states which is different from the concept of a material body. For they wish to single out sets of mental states and go on to make the nontrivial claim about each of those sets that it is dependent upon some particular body. So they cannot use the body to single out the sets. Hence, their notion of a subject of states of consciousness must be different from their notion of a material body. Otherwise their claim degenerates into the triviality that all those states of consciousness dependent upon a body are dependent upon that body, a claim too empty to be worth asserting.

I believe that this argument is sound. But it is important to note what it does and does not establish. It establishes the *logical* distinctness of subjects of consciousness and bodies. That is to say, it establishes that expressions referring to the one cannot *mean* the same as expressions referring to the other; they cannot be synonymous; the one cannot be analyzed in terms of the other. But the argument does not rule out some form of the identity theory, i.e., the claim that the *entities* which exemplify the one set of expressions are one and the same as the entities which exemplify the other.[5] Even if the expression "subject of consciousness" does not *mean* a body of a certain sort, it still might turn out that whatever is a subject of consciousness is identical with a body of a certain sort. We shall return to this issue shortly.

In rejecting the logical identity of persons (i.e., subjects of consciousness) and bodies, Strawson might be suspected of accepting dualism. But this would be a mistake. Strawson also rejects dualism, at least in the Cartesian form we have discussed it above; he rejects the view that the subject of states of consciousness is a wholly immaterial, nonphysical thing, a thing to which nothing but states of consciousness can be ascribed. His argument is as follows.[6] If someone has the concept of a subject of consciousness, then he must be willing to allow that there could be other subjects than himself, i.e., that he might be only one self among many. To have the concept of other subjects of consciousness is to be able to distinguish one from another, pick out or identify different subjects, be able to say on some occasions at least that here is one subject rather than another. (If one had no idea how to distinguish one subject from another, then one would not have the concept of *different* subjects.) Now if other subjects of consciousness were wholly immaterial, then there would be no way of distinguishing one subject from another —how could we possibly tell how many such subjects were around us right now or which subject was which? And if there was no way of distinguishing one subject from another, then, as was just pointed out, one would not have the concept of other subjects. And therefore, as was pointed out at the beginning of this argument, one would not have the concept of a subject of consciousness at all. So the Cartesian concept of the subject as wholly immaterial is without meaning.

Therefore, if we do have a concept of a subject of consciousness, as we surely do, then it can be neither merely the concept of a body (as materialism holds) nor merely the concept of an immaterial thing (as the dualist holds). It must be the concept of an entity to which both physical and mental attributions can be made. That is to say, this subject must be not only conscious but physical as well. Strawson calls entities which admit of both mental and physical attributes *persons*.

The person theory has very attractive features. It gives full weight to the distinction between mental and physical attributes, allowing them to be attributes of basically different natures. Yet it

[5] See James W. Cornman, "Strawson's 'Person,'" *Theoria*, XXX (1964), 146-47.
[6] *Individuals*, pp. 99-104.

also does justice to the fact that they seem to be attributes of one and the same subject; we say, "As he fell through space, he wondered if the parachute would ever open," not "As his body fell through space, his mind wondered if the parachute would ever open." Nor do we seem committed to that curious entity, the immaterial, extensionless thinking substance of Descartes' dualism.

What is a person? And yet, alas, there are difficulties with the person theory. These begin to emerge when we begin probing deeper into the concept of the *person* which is involved here. Strawson defines "person" very simply, as "a type of entity such that *both* predicates ascribing states of consciousness *and* predicates ascribing corporeal characteristics, a physical situation, etc. are equally applicable to a single individual of that single type." [7] But such a definition does not help us very much. That it does not comes out when we ask how the person theory differs from the identity theory.

Identity theorists wish to say that mental attributes are attributes of bodies. Furthermore, most of them wish to say that in some sense the mental attributes are reducible to physical attributes. Not all hold to the latter thesis, however. Herbert Feigl holds that where mentalistic terms are appropriate the basic and underlying reality is *mental* and physicalistic terms refer to this mental reality.[8] Thus Feigl seems to admit a dualism of attributes, mental and physical. Yet his is an identity theory both in the sense that the basic subjects of consciousness are bodies and in the sense that certain mentalistic and physicalistic terms have one and the same referent (although some of these terms will have a *mental* referent). Now Strawson would certainly reject the contention that mental attributes are reducible in any sense to physical attributes. But would he reject the claim that they are attributes of bodies? Does he wish to say that persons are bodies of a certain sort, namely bodies which have mental attributes as well?

It is clear that Strawson holds persons to be things which have bodily attributes. But that does not make them bodies any more than the fact that something has red in it makes it red. For, unlike ordinary bodies, persons are things which have mental attributes as

---

[7] *Ibid.*, p. 102.
[8] Herbert Feigl, "The 'Mental' and the 'Physical,' " *Minnesota Studies in the Philosophy of Science*, Vol. II (Minneapolis: University of Minnesota Press, 1958), pp. 474-75. The essay has recently been reprinted, under the same title, as a separate monograph (Minneapolis: University of Minnesota Press, 1967); a postscript contains Feigl's most recent thoughts on this matter. See also Feigl's contribution to Sidney Hook, ed., *Dimensions of Mind* (New York: Collier Books, 1961): "Mind-Body, Not a Pseudo-problem," pp. 33-44.

well. Furthermore, for Strawson it is not the case that persons are things which just happen to have bodily attributes (but might not have had them), nor is it the case that they are things which just happen to have mental attributes (but might not have had them). It is essential to persons, on Strawson's conception of them, that they be entities which necessarily have *both* mental and bodily attributes. And that means that they are things which differ essentially from bodies (which have only bodily attributes necessarily). They are different types of stuffs or substances or entities. And therefore the person theory is fundamentally different from materialism of any sort. It is dualistic in holding that there are two different types of subjects in the natural world, physical bodies and persons. Physical bodies necessarily have solely the physical dimension; persons necessarily have two dimensions, a physical and a mental dimension. It is the latter contention which distinguishes it from Spinoza's double aspect theory; for Spinoza, everything which exists in the world is, in Strawson's sense, a person, i.e., a thing which necessarily has both a mental and a physical dimension.

If we cannot say, on the person theory, that a person *is* a body, perhaps we can say that a person is, *in part*, a body (in the way that a thing which has red in it may be in part red). But this will not do either, for it inevitably raises the question what the rest of it is. That is, it suggests that a person is some sort of an amalgam, a compound of a body and something else (perhaps a soul?). Such suggestions are precisely what the person theory attempts to combat.

Can we even say that a person *has* a body? I suppose that Strawson would want to be able to say that. But what would it mean on the person theory? Doubtless it means that persons have bodily attributes. But does it mean any more? Is it to say anything about a relation between a person and a *body*? Not on the person theory. For a *body* is something which necessarily has solely bodily attributes and such a thing has nothing to do with persons, which, as we saw, are things which necessarily have both bodily and mental attributes.

Does very much hang on this question of the relation (on the person theory) between persons and bodies? A good deal. For example, consider the laws of nature which hold for bodies, the laws of physics, chemistry, biology. Surely we would want to be able to say that these laws are true for human bodies as well as other bodies. If it is true, in its Newtonian formulation, that "a *body* continues its state of rest or steady motion unless . . . ," we would want this to hold for the bodies of persons as well as for all other bodies. Yet if we cannot even say that a person's "body" is a *body* in the same sense that rocks and trees are bodies, then these laws of nature, which apply to *bodies*, cannot be applied to the "bodies" of persons. And that would be so great an inconvenience, to say nothing of its absurdity, as to count against the person theory.

To be sure, the term "body" is used in many ways besides the Newtonian one cited above, some of which tie better with the person theory. For example, consider the old song "Gin a body meet a body comin' thro the rye." Here of course we are not envisioning a collision of solids but an encounter between persons. In this context, the term "body" is simply used to mean a person. (Sometimes the reverse is the case. When we say "They searched his person," we are using "person" to mean a body.)

There is another use which comes even closer to the Strawsonian conception of a body. If someone said "They found a body in the lake today," we would be very surprised if he meant a rock, or a tree trunk, or an old, sunken boat, or a fish, although all of these are, in the Newtonian sense, bodies. Here "body" means "corpse," i.e., a dead human being (a dead *animal* is called a carcass rather than a corpse). A corpse or "body" in this sense is what is left when a person dies, although it is not a *part* of a living person or something which he *has* while he is alive (he does have the right to say what is to be done with it after he dies). This concept of the body becomes gruesomely explicit when we refer to it as "the remains."

It is this conception of the body which comes closest to that found in the person theory. For, in that theory, as we have seen, a body is not a person, nor is it a part of a person, nor is it something a person has. At most it is the person insofar as he is thought of as the subject of bodily attributes. It is then an abstraction, an intellectual construction, rather than a reality. But it becomes a reality at death. It materializes into that thing we call a corpse. On the person theory, a human body is what would be the person's corpse if he died; the only way we can talk about a person's body is if we consider him as if he were dead.

It is, then, one of the paradoxical implications of the person theory that the body which a person has cannot be conceived of as a physical object subject to the laws of the physical world. In its attempt to establish the unity of the person (contra dualism) without sacrificing the thesis that persons are conscious (contra materialism), the person theory seems to end with the absurdity that a person's body is not a *physical* thing.

In view of the grave difficulties in materialism and the person theory, it might be useful to review the objections to dualism and see if they can be met in some way. After all, dualism does have the advantage over materialism of accounting for the inability to reduce mental phenomena to material phenomena and the advantage over the person theory of allowing for the treatment of the human body as a material body in principle no different from other material bodies. It would be desirable to preserve these advantages, if we could overcome the disadvantages which seem to rule dualism out.

We noted that one source of discontent with dualism was that it seemed to commit us to the existence of a very peculiar kind of entity, a something which persists in time, has states, undergoes changes, and engages in processes, and yet is invisible, intangible, without size or shape or mass. What a curious something it is; it does not even seem *intelligible* that there should be such a thing. Nothing can be said about it except that it is a subject of consciousness! And that hardly makes clear what it is.

I do not think that this difficulty can be met directly. If the dualist is correct, then the notion of a nonmaterial subject of consciousness is perplexing and obscure, and nothing can be done about that. But we can weaken the force of the difficulty. It depends upon an implicit comparison of the immaterial subject of consciousness with the material subject of material states, material events, and material processes. It is suggested by this implicit comparison that the notion of the latter is clear and intelligible whereas the notion of the former is not. But it is not true that the notion of a material thing is clear and intelligible. We can raise parallel objections to it. We may ask of a material thing which has states, undergoes changes, and engages in processes, *What is it* which has these states, undergoes changes, and engages in processes? What *is* a material thing? On reflection we will see that the only thing which can be said is that it is a something which is the subject of certain sorts of states, events, and processes, namely material ones. Nothing more can be said than that. But precisely that sort of thing, no more and no less, can be said of an immaterial thing, namely that it is a something which is the subject of certain sorts of states, events, and processes, namely ones involving consciousness. So in this respect, immaterial things are no worse off than material things.

However, we are still left with two particular problems here, which we referred to earlier as the problem of identification and the problem of individuation (see pp. 38-39, above).

So far as identification is concerned, it does seem to be the case that we can only tell we are in the presence of another consciousness and can only tell whose consciousness it is by observing *physical* phenomena. We have no way of getting at the other mind directly. Of course, the problem of identification would be easier if mental telepathy were a common phenomenon. Then one could communicate with another mind without resort to ordinary sense observation and one might tell, by the content of the communication, whom one was communicating with. Thus if it communicated information which only your uncle could know, that would be good reason to think it was your uncle you were in communication with. There is some question even here how much such inferences are based upon what we know about the world through sense observation; for example, you would think it was something only your uncle could know because you know, perhaps, that only he was in the room at the time (as established by observing, through the window, his body and the otherwise empty room). So if in the end sense observation must be depended upon, telepathy will not help. But even if it did help it is not available to us for determining the identity of other consciousnesses. So we must depend upon sense observations of material bodies, especially human bodies. And that leaves mental things in a weaker position, at least epistemologically, than material things.

So far as individuation is concerned, too, mental entities seem to have a weaker status than material entities. For it does seem to be possible for there to be two different persons who have exactly the same mental history, exactly the same set of mental states and events throughout their life. The only thing that could distinguish the two would be the existence of different bodies in different places (although having exactly similar mental histories would necessitate their having exactly similar bodies and environments). This indicates that mental entities depend in part on material entities for their individuation.

We must conclude that any theory of the nature of the subject of consciousness must include some reference to material bodies, although it may not be necessary to *identify* the subject of consciousness with the material body. Indeed, we have seen that there are grave difficulties in attempts to defend such an identification. Yet a dualism which includes the concept of an immaterial subject of consciousness utterly independent of material bodies is unable to deal with the problems of identification and individuation. So we must turn to a closer look at the relation of consciousness and the body. That is the task of the following chapter.

CONSCIOUSNESS

AND THE BODY

4

From what we have seen so far in this book, it is unlikely that we will be able to "reduce" the phenomena of consciousness to physical phenomena; that is, it is unlikely that we will be able to show either that consciousness is *definable* in terms of the physical or to show that it is in fact *identical* with the physical. If that is the case, then we must face the problem of how the two phenomena are related, if they are related at all. That is the task of this chapter.

It would seem to be a familiar fact that states of consciousness can be produced, eliminated, or modified by physical changes. (We will soon see that this apparently "familiar fact" is open to various interpretations.) Consider visual phenomena. By covering the eyes we can eliminate or at least sharply curtail visual content, and by uncovering them we can restore it. We can cause ourselves to see double by pushing at the hollow under the eye. We can produce spots before the eyes or afterimages by looking at certain things for certain lengths of time. Illnesses like jaundice make things look different, i.e., yellowish. We know that flashes of light may be seen when we bump our heads severely or suffer a migraine attack or an epileptic seizure. Marijuana and mescaline may make things look as if they were glowing or moving; and whiskey may make it look as if the bugs were crawling up our legs again. Similar examples of physical causation can be cited for other states of consciousness, such as having sensations, emotional feelings, thoughts, images, etc. It would seem to be a familiar fact, then, that physical phenomena can affect mental phenomena.

It would also seem to be a familiar fact that mental phenomena can affect the physical world in various ways. My feeling of great terror may cause me to turn ashen, tremble, or fall down in a faint. My having the thought that it is too dark to read may lead me to turn on the lights. My "seeing bugs" may cause me to scream. My decision to start a fire may lead to the destruction of the whole city.

These, then, are apparently familiar facts which indicate an intimate relation between consciousness and physical phenomena. Since the physical phenomena most directly relevant are states and changes in the *body* (it is through our bodies that external physical phenomena affect our consciousness and it affects them), we can ignore the physical changes in the rest of the world and confine our attention to the relation between consciousness and the *body*.

Dualistic theories The most obvious theory to describe the "facts" as we have stated them is known as psychophysical interactionism. It holds that (1) states of consciousness can be causally affected by states of the body and (2) states of the body can be causally affected by states of consciousness; thus the mind and the body can interact. The paragraphs above contain respective illustrations of the two kinds of causal action.

Why have we hedged by speaking of "apparently familiar facts"? Because it is not absolutely clear that the facts are as we have stated them. Consider the "fact" that we can affect visual experience by covering the eyes. What do we really know in such cases? We know that when the eyes get covered, visual content becomes curtailed, and that when the covering is removed, visual content is restored. In other words, we know that there is a *correlation* between covering the eyes and curtailing visual content. Similarly for the second set of "facts" above, such as that my feeling of terror causes me to turn ashen. We know that when a person feels great terror, certain physical changes like turning ashen, trembling, or falling down in a faint are often correlated with it. In general we know that usually or always, depending upon the case, a particular state of consciousness is correlated with a particular physical state. But do we know any more than that? Do we know that one is the *cause* of the other?

There are two main rivals to interactionism, and each proposes a somewhat different interpretation of the "facts." Psychophysical parallelism accepts the fact of correlation but denies that there is any direct causal action between the mental and the physical; there is *mere* correlation. The following analogy is often proposed: if there were two clocks, each keeping perfect time, then each state of the one would always be *correlated* with a corresponding state of the other, but neither would in any way *cause* the other.

The other rival to interactionism is epiphenomenalism, the theory that there is a causal connection, but that it goes one way, from the physical to the mental but not from the mental to the physical. Mental states and events, on this theory, are nothing but by-products or side-effects of physical processes and themselves can have no effect on those physical processes. Physical phenomena are like the fingers moving in front of a light source and mental phenomena are like the shadows cast on the wall, produced by the moving fingers but unable to affect those fingers in any way.

Why have some philosophers turned to one of these rather curious theories rather than accept at face value the apparent fact of interaction? We will consider each of these alternative theories in turn.

Parallelism   Proponents of parallelism have refused to allow that there could be a *causal* connection between events which differ so radically in type. So they theorize that there is the kind of *correlation without direct causal connection* which we have in the case of the two perfect clocks. At the heart of this issue is the concept of *cause*. It would be nice if we could start off by giving a definition of "cause" and proceed from there, but there does not exist at present an adequate definition of that term. David Hume claimed that constant conjunction was *all* there was, objectively speaking, but that does not seem adequate, as the example of the two clocks shows. In that example we can distinguish between the constant (but *accidental*) correlation of the various phases of the *two* clocks and the constant (but *causally* connected) correlation of the successive phases in *each individual* clock. And the parallelist himself, like his rival theorists, accepts the distinction between constant correlation and causal connection; he allows causal connection between successive physical events and between successive mental events, although he rejects causal connection between physical and mental events.

Some philosophers, following a further suggestion of Hume's, hold that the cause must be at least a necessary condition. This idea can be expressed negatively and counterfactually as follows: "If the first object had not been, the second never had existed" either.[1] But this is refuted by the existence of "back-up systems" which ensure that if a result is not brought about in one way then the same result

[1] David Hume, *An Inquiry Concerning Human Understanding*, Sec. 7, Pt. 2.

will be brought about in another way; a simple example of this is leaving your car on a downhill slope in "Park" with the emergency brake on and with the front wheels jammed against the curb. In such cases, if the actual cause had not existed, the same result would still have been brought about. So the cause is not a necessary condition for the effect.

The best we can say is that to call one event the cause of the other is to say that the first is a *sufficient* condition for the second, in the sense that if the former occurs, then, given the circumstances, the latter *must* occur. But such an account does not get us anywhere, for we would still have to say what kind of "must" is involved here. It is obviously not the logical "must," which states that the occurrence of the former logically entails the occurrence of the latter. The most that can be said is that it is the causal "must," which brings us back to where we began. And that is pretty much where the analysis of causality is at the present time.

At any rate, proponents of parallelism accept the concept of causality. They allow that there is causal connection between bodily events, so that a bodily event like a cut on the hand could produce another *bodily* state, for example, stimulation in the nerves leading from the hand to the brain. And they allow that one *mental* event, say, feeling a sharp pain, could affect another *mental* event, say, the thought that I'd better do something about that pain. But they deny that a *physical* event like the stimulation of certain nerves, a public matter of electrochemical occurrences in tiny cells, could produce a *mental* event like a sensation of pain, private to the individual concerned and utterly different in character from electrochemical cellular phenomena. And similarly, they deny that a mental event like a sensation of pain could produce an electrochemical change in cells. The events in question are so utterly dissimilar, they argue, that it is inconceivable that events of one type should produce events of the other type.

It might be thought that the present difference in kind between the mental and physical will be closed by future physiological or psychological discoveries of some sort of "bridge" between the mental and the physical. But it must be admitted that that is a pipe dream. All that we can expect from future research is a more precise determination of the mental and physical events involved. We will still be left with the basic difference in type between some sort of mental event on the one hand and some sort of physical event on the other. And that would still leave us with the problem how such different sorts of events could affect each other.

The hypothesis of psychophysical parallelism presents rather considerable problems of its own, however. The situation with respect to the two clocks, the basic analogy of parallelism, is clear enough; each clock has its own internal mechanism which accounts for its own successive states, and the perfection of each mechanism keeps the two always in phase. But the situation in the case of mind and body does not seem analogous. For while there may be a way of accounting for the various succeeding states of the body in purely physical terms, there does not seem to be a way of accounting for the various succeeding states of the mind in purely mental terms. Consider a person asleep who is awakened by a fire alarm. His mind is suddenly filled with a wailing, clamorous noise. Now if the parallelist is right, the occurrence of that mental event, the hearing of the noise, can be explained simply within the realm of mental events, by some prior mental event. But surely hearing that wailing noise cannot be explained simply by appealing to some prior mental state or event. The only obvious candidate for the prior cause of the hearing is the ringing of the alarm, and that is ruled out as a cause on the parallelist thesis. So all that the parallelist can say of this case is that when the alarm rings, then at the same time there just happens to be the accompanying mental event of the hearing of the alarm and that this is a mere correlation without causal connection. But then it is *completely inexplicable* why that correlation should occur, whereas in the case of the two clocks it was entirely explicable why the correlations should occur. So the analogy breaks down here. The mental does not comprise a self-enclosed and causally self-sufficient system in the way that each clock in the analogy does. Therefore on the parallelist theory the undeniable fact of correlation of mental and physical is left completely miraculous and inexplicable.

In attempting to deal with this difficulty, the French seventeenth century philosopher Malebranche introduced a theory (called occasionalism) to the effect that, on the occasion when the alarm rings, *God* produces in the mind the hearing of the alarm. But this desperate attempt to explain the correlation of mental and physical without resorting to direct causal action between them has never appealed to the modern mind. There is not much difference between saying that the correlation which exists between the ringing of the alarm and the hearing of that ringing is totally inexplicable and saying that the correlation is miraculously produced by the action of the divine will.

Why does the parallelist resist what seems to be so obvious a conclusion, namely that the ringing *causes* the hearing? Because the events involved are so utterly different in their natures. But what is the source of this resistance? After all, are there not many cases in which the cause and effect differ utterly? Consider a very cold piece of ice which is gradually heated, so that we eventually turn it from ice to a liquid to a gas. Here we have the *same* cause throughout, the application of heat. First we have the effect that the ice melts into water; then that the water increases in temperature; then that the water begins to boil; then that the water begins to vaporize; and then that the vapor increases in temperature. How utterly different these effects are one from the other and how utterly different each is from the cause! Yet it would be rash indeed to say that there can be no causal connection, only correlation, because the alleged cause and effects are so different from each other. Cause and effect are where we find them, and it would be in violation of the principles of scientific reasoning if we rejected some apparent causal connections on the a priori ground that the events were "too different" to be causally connected.

Why might a person be inclined to think that the difference in type between mental events and physical events would rule out a causal connection? One possible source of this inclination is the feeling that there should be some sort of *intelligible connection* between the cause and the effect, that one should be able to discern in the cause the coming of the effect, that the effect should be contained in the cause in some way and should emerge forth from the cause. This feeling is strongly present in Spinoza, a classic case of a philosopher who denied the possibility of interaction between the mental and the physical. He held that the effect follows from the cause in the way that the propositions in a geometrical system follow from the definitions and axioms and therefore that "if two things have nothing in common with one another, one cannot be the cause of the other."[2] On such reasoning it becomes plausible to hold that the mental and physical cannot causally affect each other.

It was Hume who pointed out with such force that this picture of causality is incorrect. He maintained that no scrutiny of the cause, no matter how searching, would tell us prior to experience what the effect would be. It is only by waiting to see what happens that we can determine what causes give rise to what effects. After a suitable amount of experience we may be able to infer from the existence of a particular event that it will have a particular effect, but such an inference is based merely on the knowledge that in the past the two have been correlated. And if events of two kinds have

[2] *Ethics*, Part I, Prop. III.

been correlated in the past, then it becomes likely that they are causally related, no matter how different in character they may be.

Some philosophers have rejected theories positing a causal relation between mental and physical events on the grounds that such a relation would violate the principle of conservation of mass-energy, a cornerstone of contemporary physical science. If physical events produced mental effects, then in so doing energy would be expended and the total mass-energy of the physical system would be reduced. And if mental events produced physical changes, then the total mass-energy of the physical system would be increased. In either case the conservation principle would be violated. And, it is argued, it would be more rational to reject any such theory than to reject the conservation principle. Is this objection to causal theories valid?

Defenders of interactionist theories have sometimes maintained that in the long run things would even out, that the energy lost in producing mental effects would be gained back from mental causes. Other interactionists and epiphenomenalists have sometimes maintained that the amount of energy gained or lost might well be so slight as to be negligible for all practical and experimental purposes. But such moves will not work, for two reasons. First, there is not the slightest reason to believe they are true; if energy is not conserved in the physical system, then there is no reason to think the long-run total is conserved or only minutely altered. Second, we would still be required to abandon the conservation principle as it is currently held; and since so much of contemporary physics, with all its incredibly fruitful developments, depends upon this principle, that would be most undesirable.

Both of these attempted defenses of causal theories admit more to the objection than they should. They admit that, in an interaction between the mental and the physical, physical energy would be gained or lost. But that is a mistake. Physical energy is gained or lost, according to contemporary physical theory, only in *physical* interactions. It takes physical energy to do *physical* work, but there is no reason to think that it takes physical energy to do nonphysical (i.e., mental) work. Similarly, there is no reason to think that nonphysical causality necessarily changes the physical energy level.

Let us consider two examples of how causal interaction could occur without changes in energy. First, for mental events as causes, consider the emission of a particle from a piece of radioactive material. Energy is conserved whether the emission occurs now or a little earlier or later, although the total effects could be quite different depending upon the time of emission. Now suppose it is a *mental* event which determines the time of emission! That would in no way affect the total energy of the system, although it could greatly alter the future history of the system. Some interactionists have speculated that mental events could affect so-called "random" occurrences in brain neurons and thereby significantly affect the total behavior of the organism. Second, for mental events as effects, consider the changing shadows cast by objects. No extra energy is lost producing the changes in the shadows over and above the energy lost in moving the objects, light sources, and shaded surfaces. The events which consist in changes in the shadows do not require further energy for their production. One can think of some changes in the mental realm as changes projected on the mental "surface" by physical interactions. No further work would be required for that, and therefore no energy would be lost in such an action.

We can conclude that the conservation principle offers no objection to causal theories, any more than does the fact that mental events and physical events are so very different in character.

It therefore is unreasonable to admit the correlation between mental events and physical events and yet still deny that there is any causal connection between them. It is true that correlations can be explained in various ways other than by postulating a direct causal connection. The case of the two clocks is one such way. But, as we have seen, that kind of alternative explanation is not available in the case of the mental and the physical.

Another alternative to direct causal connection should be mentioned here. It is based on an analogy to the following kind of case. Imagine some irreversible process, an incurable disease, for example, which always has one symptom at an early stage and another symptom at a later stage. In such a case there would be a constant conjunction between the earlier and the later symptom, but there would be no direct causal connection between them. The earlier would not cause the later but rather each would be caused by some third thing, the underlying pathological condition. In similar fashion one might conceive of the mental and physical as constantly correlated by virtue of some underlying third thing which produces each of them. A view very much like this was held by Spinoza. And it is possible that the view we discussed in Chapter 3 under the name of the person theory might be another variant of such a conception. Such a view would resemble parallelism in denying direct causal connection but differ from it in postulating an indirect causal connection via the underlying third thing.

The only trouble with such a view is that there is no reason at all to believe it. There is no reason to believe there is some third thing which underlies both the mental and the physical and can explain the sequence of events in each. Such a unified theory may become plausible at some future time, but at the present it has no support. Spinoza referred to his third thing variously as Substance, God, and Nature, but he offered no evidence to show that such a thing could indeed explain the sequence of mental and physical events. And no one else has been able to make out a plausible case for the existence of some third thing which underlies and accounts for both the mental and the physical. Let us turn, then, to the theories which do allow for direct causal connection between mental and physical events. Namely, epiphenomenalism and interactionism.

Epiphe-   The epiphenomenalist holds that there is a causal connection
nomenalism   between the mental and the physical but that it only goes in one direction, from the physical to the mental, so that mental events always are the *effects* of physical changes and never are *causes* of physical changes. Mental events are, as it were, a shadow cast by physical processes and incapable of affecting those physical processes. The epiphenomenalist accepts the first set of familiar facts indicated at the beginning of this chapter, an example of which is that we can causally affect visual content by a physical change like covering the eyes. But he rejects what seems to be an equally familiar set of facts in which mental events causally affect the physical. Why?

The epiphenomenalist believes that a consideration of the development of the physical sciences will show a steady increase in the number of physical phenomena which can be explained in purely physical terms. In case after case, the postulation of non-physical causes of physical phenomena has proved fruitless, whereas the postulation of physical causes has yielded important results. We no longer believe that immaterial spirits affect the weather, the productivity of crops, or animal fertility; we can explain these in purely physical terms. We have found that kinds of abnormal behavior, e.g., epileptic seizures, are caused by brain malfunctioning; we no longer need appeal to possesssion by demons. And ghosts, poltergeists, and other spirits no longer play the role they used to in explanation of physical phenomena. It is not an unreasonable extrapolation to postulate that the *whole* of physical phenomena is, in the end, explicable in purely physical terms. This seems to be the direction in which science is moving. We may never come to the time when we can, in fact, explain everything in purely physical terms, but, argues the epiphenomenalist, there is no reason to think that there is some nonphysical agency which must be postulated to explain any physical phenomena. And the whole history of science goes against such postulations.

But what does the epiphenomenalist make of the apparently familiar cases in which the mental seems to affect the physical? A man cuts his hand and the feeling of pain, we are inclined to say, causes him to wince. For the epiphenomenalist what really happens is this. The cut produces a series of events in the nerves which lead to his brain, resulting in the occurrence of a *brain* state which causes the physical movement we call a wince. That brain state also causes the sensation we call the feeling of pain; the sensation is merely a *by-product* of a chain of physical events, which starts with the cut and ends with the wince; in itself the sensation has no effect on any part of the series. Similarly for my thought that it is too dark to read, which ostensibly causes me to turn on the light. It is a mere by-product of a purely physical causal sequence which starts with a particular physical stimulation of my sense organs, produces a particular brain state, and results in my hand moving out and turning on the light; the thought itself has no effects on the sequence of physical events. It is an *illusion* that mental events have effects, just as it is an illusion that the moving hands of a clock cause the clock to strike the hour.

The paradox of epiphe- nomenalism If it is only an *illusion* that mental events have effects, then human affairs must be conceived quite differently from the way they are ordinarily conceived. Historians like to attribute events to human decisions, emotions, thoughts, and sensations. All of that would be in error on this theory. And our ordinary, every-day explanations of human behavior in those terms would also be in error. The epiphenomenalist would have us believe that the Pyramids and the Empire State Building were erected without the aid of a single thought, that the greatest works of art were created without the effect of a single feeling, that wars have been declared and nuclear weapons employed, but not as the result of a single human deliberation or decision. Since his view is that mental events have no consequences, the epiphenomenalist would have us believe that the whole of human history would have developed in just the way that it did even if there had never been a single thought, feel-ing, sensation, decision, or other mental event. Everything would have gone on just the same, even if *everyone had always been com-*

pletely unconscious. Even our language, with all its mentalistic expressions, would have existed, and, most astonishing of all, all the verbal interchanges which represent our discussions about the very existence and nature of mental events would have occurred. If there had never been a mental event, men still would have believed in their existence, or if belief itself is a mental phenomenon, men still would have spoken and acted as if there were mental events!

Many philosophers have found these paradoxical implications of epiphenomenalism too incredible to accept. Yet they must be accepted if epiphenomenalism is correct. For, on that theory, mental events themselves have no consequences, produce no effects, and nothing else would have been different if they had never occurred. They are, in the words of a twentieth century epiphenomenalist, George Santayana, "a lyric cry in the midst of business" and a cry which could in no way affect the course of business.

In all fairness to the epiphenomenalist position, it must be pointed out that the theory is not quite so incredible as it appears; the appearance of wild paradox can be to some degree dissipated. When the epiphenomenalist says that all would have gone on in exactly the same way even if no man had ever been conscious, he is not suggesting that the Pyramids could have been built by men in their sleep, or in deep comas, or in profound swoons, or with vacant stares. And when he says that they could have done these things without thoughts, feelings, decisions, etc., he is not suggesting that they did them impulsively, numbly, or at random. We must picture men moving skillfully about, poring over plans, scratching their heads or resting them on their hands, gesticulating animatedly—in short, men behaving with the full range of that behavior which is typical of consciousness. What any observer would see if he were to witness the scene would be exactly the same as what he would see in the actual case where men do have mental events. The only thing left out would be the mental events. And since they are private and invisible, their absence would never be noticed. So we are not envisioning anything so paradoxical after all.

If we concluded that epiphenomenalism is true, would we have to stop saying such things as "The pain made him scream" or "He screamed from the pain," remarks which appear pointedly interactionistic? It might be argued that we could continue truthfully to say such things, understanding them to mean the same as the more theoretically neutral remark, "*He screamed with pain.*" After all, a sympathizer might argue, we still say "The sun set at 6 P.M.," even if we no longer accept the Ptolemaic view that the sun moves around the earth. But I think it would be a mistake to argue in this way. For "The sun set at 6 P.M." is *genuinely neutral* between astronomical theories; it simply describes the vanishing of the sun from view, and does not commit one to an explanation of that vanishing by virtue of the relative movement of the earth and the sun or the rotational movement of the earth upon its axis. But "The pain made him scream" is not neutral in the same way. It says clearly and explicitly that the feeling causes the behavior. And if epiphenomenalism turns out to be true, then this expression of ordinary language is simply false; plain men might continue to use it but they would always be wrong when they did.

Psychophysical interactionism How does epiphenomenalism compare with its primary rival, interactionism? Interactionism agrees with epiphenomenalism in holding that physical occurrences can have mental effects, but goes beyond it by holding in addition that *mental occurrences can have physical effects.* Thus the interactionist accepts as genuine fact the apparent facts cited at the beginning of this chapter; it thereby comes closest to the commonsense view of the man in the street (and that is neither in its favor nor against it). But we have seen that these "facts" which seem to establish interaction are actually open to either an epiphenomenalist or interactionist interpretation.

In trying to decide between these two theories the crucial question to be determined is whether mental events ever have effects. Now, there is a difficulty which arises in trying to answer that question which does *not* arise when we try to determine whether *physical* events can have mental effects. We can, by experiment, introduce an exclusively physical change and see whether it has mental effects or not. For example, we can ring a bell and determine that the ringing affects a person's body and subsequently produces the mental event which consists in the person's hearing the bell. We can show beyond a reasonable doubt that both the physical bodily effects and the mental effects were caused by the physical event of ringing the bell. And thus we can answer conclusively by experiment the question whether physical events can have mental effects. But whether mental events can be causes and have effects is more difficult to determine. It would be easy if we could introduce an exclusively mental change and see whether it has effects; if this exclusively mental change were followed by events which could be explained only by appeal to that mental change, then that would show that mental events can be causes. But, unfortunately, we cannot set up an experimental situation in which it is clear that we have produced an exclusively mental change. The only mental events we can experimentally manipulate are those of creatures having complex and ever active nervous systems. Any mental change will be accompanied by innumerable concomitant physical changes in the nervous system. So even if the mental change were followed by some other event it would always be open to the epiphenomenalist to say that the subsequent event had been produced not by the mental event but by some *physical* event concomitant with that mental event. For example, suppose we produce the consciousness of pain which is followed by a wince; how could it be known that it was the *mental* event of feeling pain rather than the brain events concomitant with the consciousness of pain which produced the wince?

This is not to say that we may never settle the matter. At some future time, when we know a great deal more about the brain than we do now, we may be able to determine whether the mental event or some concomitant brain event was the cause. Let us consider the following case: I am puzzling over a difficult arithmetic problem and suddenly the solution flashes across my mind (a mental event). Then I start writing down the solution (a physical event). Suppose it turns out that while I am puzzling over the problem my brain is in an indeterminate state, idling, as it were, so that no future state could be predicted from its present state. Then the solution dawns on me. *Subsequently* the brain goes into that state which produces the muscular activity of writing down the solution. If this were to happen, it would be reasonable to think that the mental event caused the physical one. Under these circumstances, interaction would be vindicated. Of course, the epiphenomenalist might hold out for a long time, saying that the brain was not really in the indeterminate state and that, if we searched longer we would find the *brain* events which caused the subsequent physical events. But in time it could be shown that such a position was mere dogmatism.

But there is no reason to believe that such future discoveries will actually be made. We simply do not know anywhere near enough as yet about brain functionings to have the slightest information one way or the other. We will just have to wait for future developments in neurophysiology.

An afterlife?   A relevant question here is whether there is any continued existence of the person's conscious life in a disembodied form after the death of the body. For a consciousness to continue to have mental events without a body would show that mental events are not merely a byproduct of bodily processes. That would refute epiphenomenalism, although it would not establish interactionism; we would still need evidence that this disembodied consciousness could affect the physical. If, even in disembodied form, it could not affect the physical, then consciousness might be like a barge which can do nothing but follow its tug, and, when the towline breaks, can only toss helplessly at the mercy of any chance current. And even if this disembodied consciousness could affect the physical world, that in itself would not establish mind-*body* interaction, since it might turn out to be the case that consciousness could affect the physical *only* in a disembodied state and not when the person had a body. Still, such disembodied causal powers, if they exsited, would make the hypothesis of mind-body interaction more likely. (It should be noted that the occurrence of transmigration, the passage of a consciousness from one body to another, would not have any relevance in the issue between these two theories; it would be compatible with either of them.)

Such a survival of consciousness after the death of the body certainly is imaginable, at least in one's own case. I suddenly feel an intense pain in my chest, I feel myself falling, and everything goes black. And then I seem to see the following: people bending over a body which appears to be mine, a doctor feeling for a pulse, an ambulance arriving, the doctor saying it is too late, and my body taken away. I no longer see anything which could be a body which belongs to me; for example, I seem to look straight into a mirror, but cannot see any human figures at all. Later I watch a funeral, hear people say kind things about me, see weeping. All during this time I have thoughts, sense impressions, feelings. I continue to be conscious, but no longer have a body. Surely this is intelligible.

But imaginable as it is, is there any reason to think that disembodied existence ever has occurred? This question is, of course, of the greatest personal importance, and has been discussed about as much as any other topic one can think of. People have very strong feelings about it, one way or the other. But the fact is that, by the nature of the hypothesis, it is almost impossible to get good evidence for either side.

What is the evidence in favor of disembodied survival? There are many reports of messages from people who have apparently died, messages containing information which presumably only the "deceased" knew. Unfortunately, such cases always admit of other possible explanations than that the "deceased" is still somehow in existence in disembodied form. There has never been a scientifically controlled experiment that was very persuasive in its results. It would have to be something on the order of that of the famous magician and escape artist Houdini, who arranged for a friend to visit his grave on each anniversary of his death to receive a prearranged message. After twenty-five fruitless years, his friend finally gave up his annual visit to Houdini's grave. If the message had come through, that would have had some relevance in showing the survival of consciousness. What is the evidence against disembodied survival? We know that many mental functionings are affected adversely by brain damage and that the greater the damage the worse the effect. By extrapolation it might well be expected that when, in bodily death, there is complete cessation of brain functioning, there would also be complete cessation of mental functioning. Some philosophers, in defending the survival hypothesis, have argued that such brain deterioration may decrease not mental functioning itself but only the ability of the ill patient to communicate his mental events to others. But such a defense will not do. There are cases where the brain condition has improved, and the testimony of such patients does not support the claim that merely the ability to communicate was affected.

But unfortunately for the argument from extrapolation, one cannot tell whether extrapolation is justified in this case; it is possible that at death consciousness is suddenly "freed" from bodily dependence and resumes its fullness of function. So the argument is by no means conclusive. Yet extrapolation is a legitimate scientific procedure in general, and there is no reason to think it is unjustified here. So, although the issue is still very much an open one, the weight of evidence at present seems to go against the hypothesis of survival. Furthermore, there is a sort of negative evidence against survival. If there were such a thing, would it not be likely that there would be more positive evidence for it than there is? Would we not expect more in the way of messages from these disembodied survivors? Is not lack of such evidence further reason to think that it does not exist, or, at the least, if it does exist, that it is powerless to affect the physical world? So here we have further reason, albeit not very conclusive, to reject the hypothesis of survival after the death of the body.

Parapsychological phenomena   There are many people, including some philosophers and scientific researchers, who believe in the existence of a kind of occurrence which would count in favor of interactionism and against epiphenomenalism. Such alleged occurrences are called parapsychological phenomena, and they are studied by men who call themselves parapsychologists.

Mental telepathy would be an example of this sort of occurrence. It is a case of direct communication of some thought from one mind to another without any intervening physical interaction. A typical experimental situation would be the following: A "sender" concentrates on a series of playing cards, one by one, and a "receiver," in another room or even in another country, tries to say what the series is. The intervening distances and shielding devices are varied as much as possible to rule out any physical interaction between the two bodies. Now suppose that the "receiver" gets a higher proportion of correct answers than chance would allow. Then it becomes plausible to maintain that there is some sort of causal interaction between the two. If the better than chance result is unaffected by variations in distance or shielding devices, then it becomes plausible to maintain that the causal interaction is directly between minds rather than via some physical medium. Such an occurrence would go against the epiphenomenalist, who maintains that mental events can have no effects.

Another example would be psychokinesis, the mental affecting the physical. A typical experimental situation would be the following: We drop thousands of dice, and a group of persons concentrates on, say, the number six. Again we vary the intervening distances and shielding devices to rule out physical interaction between the bodies and the dice. Suppose that we get a higher proportion of sixes than chance would allow. Then it becomes plausible to maintain that the mental event of concentrating has an effect on the physical dice-tossing. This would confirm interactionism.

It would be open to a dedicated supporter of epiphenomenalism to claim that the interaction was indeed physical but involved some kind of unknown force or energy which was invariant with respect to distance and penetrated all known shields. But that would be a move of desperation. For such a "force" would be so unlike anything falling under the present physical laws that it could hardly be called a *physical* phenomenon at all. And even if we called it "physical," it would give epiphenomenalism merely the illusory appearance of victory, since the "physical" would now contain within itself two utterly different kinds of phenomena, and we would still be left with the dualistic question of the relation between them. So nothing would have been gained by this essentially verbal maneuver.

Is there any reason to think that mental telepathy and psychokinesis do in fact occur? The vast majority of scientists do not think so, but it must be said that very few of them have actually considered the experimental evidence in detail. For most it is a prejudice, dogmatically held, that there cannot be such phenomena as mental telepathy or psychokinesis. Of those scientists who have gone carefully into the matter, some think there may be something here, some do not. The most that can be said is that no one has yet been able to show decisively that such phenomena do occur. So we cannot look here for help in judging between epiphenomenalism and inter-actionism.

Other parapsychological phenomena would be relevant too, of course. Messages from departed souls, poltergeist phenomena, effica-cious prayers, dreams that forecast the as yet unknown, and seeing into the future or the past might well count toward establishing the interactionist thesis. But the lack of controlled experiments and ob-jective observation in alleged instances of these phenomena make the case here even weaker than for telepathy or psychokinesis. There may turn out to be important phenomena occuring here, but anecdotes and folklore do not go very far in providing solid evidence for it.

If we cannot look to present-day neurophysiology or parapsy-chology for help, must we remain completely on the fence with re-spect to epiphenomenalism and interactionism? There is one rather indirect consideration which, I think, has some weight in tipping the scale toward epiphenomenalism. We have very good reason to be-lieve that brain events themselves have causal effects, both on sub-sequent brain events and on mental events, and we can produce controlled experiments to show that. We know, for example, that stimulating the brain can produce subsequent mental events and subsequent brain events. So far, the developments in neurophysi-ology have consisted of discovering more and more cases in which brain events are causes. And we have every reason to believe that future developments in that field will be consistent with this trend, so that eventually we can assume, by extrapolation, that all brain events and concomitant mental events will be explainable in terms of brain events. On the other hand, we have no experimental evi-dence to show that *mental* events, by themselves, ever affect other mental events or brain events, and we have no reason to think that future developments will give us such evidence. Perhaps it is more reasonable to believe that scientific developments will continue in the direction they have moved in the past than to believe that a radically new kind of causal agent will be discovered and experi-mentally verified. And that means that perhaps it is more reasonable to accept epiphenomenalism than to believe in interactionism, with its utterly gratuitous postulation of a presently groundless mental causality.

ACTIONS

5

A man is in the forest gathering wood for a fire. Scattered all about him in the forest are pieces of wood. To give the full account of how those pieces of wood got there would be to know how the nebulae were formed, how the earth cooled, how plants evolved, how seeds blow in the wind, and how the floodwaters flow. The processes of nature work on, impartially and consistently producing their changes in the production and distribution of natural things. But a few of these pieces of wood now scattered about have a special destiny. They will be singled out by the man, carried by him to a place they would never have occupied, to meet a fate he has designed for them and will deliberately carry out. This man, through his action, has intervened in nature: "By action we irreducibly alter the state of the universe; a form or pattern appears that was not there before, the existence of which does not seem to follow in any way from the physical state of the universe beforehand. This is creation." [1] But if we ask ourselves what this "creation" is, what an *action* is, it is not so easy to say. Our problem is this: How, if at all, are our actions significantly different from the rest of the changes that occur in nature?

It is a useful beginning to note that human beings and the higher animals can move about from place to place "on their own," and move other things also. Rocks and flowers, when they do move

[1] Brian O'Shaughnessy, "Observation and the Will," *The Journal of Philosophy*, LX, No. 14 (July 4, 1963), 368.

from place to place, are impelled by other things, whereas human beings are *self-movers* who initiate and direct their own movements.

However, when we consider that there do exist *self-propelled* inanimate things, of which rockets are a recent dramatic example, we must make some modifications in this view. For it is plain that an inanimate object may contain within itself the energy for its own movement and perhaps even something which controls the direction of its movement. So if we are going to come up with a distinction here between human beings and the higher animals on the one hand and plants and inanimate objects on the other, self-movement alone will not serve to make the distinction.

Perhaps we can make the following distinction. The movements of human beings (and other animals) are often *actions* which the agent performs *intentionally*, whereas plants and inanimate things are merely passive objects which are acted upon. Human beings can do things and make things happen on purpose; they are not merely things *to which* things happen. Human beings can deliberately *control* their movements; plants and inanimate things cannot. Not even our self-propelled rocket can act *intentionally*.

Of course, even human beings are sometimes merely passive things which are acted upon, and at such times this alleged difference between human beings and lower nature is not apparent. For example, we watch with horror as a man falls from the tenth story of a building. As he falls, the forces acting upon him make him fall at an accelerating speed; they are precisely the same as those which would act upon an inanimate dummy. So far as the falling is concerned, the man and the dummy do not differ in any important way. Even if we turn to how it is that the man happened to be falling, a difference still may not emerge. The man might have been pushed from the window by a powerful force which he could not resist and which would have had exactly the same effect on an inanimate dummy. But, and here a difference does seem to emerge, the man might have *jumped* from the window intentionally and of his own will, as an agent who performed the action on his own. In such a case, his falling was not something which happened to him; it was something he intentionally made happen. Naturally, once he jumped, his continued falling was something which happened to him beyond his control, but nevertheless he brought the falling about by his act of jumping from the window. Even though he could not stop the falling once it began, it was he who initiated it.

One might think that the essence of the difference between jumping out the window intentionally and being pushed out consists in whether the cause of the movement was internal or external. But this would be an oversimplification. For there are many human movements that have an internal cause but that we would *not* say are voluntary and intentional actions under the control of the agent. For example, there are tremors of the hand, twitches and tics, and the violent movements associated with epileptic seizures; these have inner causes, but they are things which happen to the person rather than things which the person actively does.

As with so many philosophical matters, an apparent difference, so obvious to common sense, turns out to be difficult to analyze. We shall see that it is extremely hard to say what does distinguish intentional actions. There will even be those who deny there is any special phenomenon at all here. This often happens in philosophy: when it is difficult to say what the difference is, it becomes tempting to deny there is any difference at all. But there certainly seems to be a difference between a hand which moves because it is pushed or because of a muscular spasm and a hand which moves because a person intentionally moves it, even if we cannot agree wherein the difference lies.

Of course, even if we can agree wherein the difference lies, it may well turn out that the difference is not very *important*. That result would have great consequences for the philosophy of mind, for being capable of performing intentional actions is often held to be one of the distinguishing features of creatures with *minds*. And so, if there is no important difference between intentional actions and non-intentional movements, then to that extent there is no important difference between creatures with mind and mindless things. Furthermore, if there is no important difference here, there are great consequences for moral philosophy as well. We do not speak of plants and inanimate objects as *moral* creatures, who *ought* to do certain things and refrain from doing others, who do *wrong* if they do what they are supposed to refrain from doing, who should be held *responsible* for what they do, and who may be *praiseworthy* if they do the right thing and *blameworthy* if they do the wrong. We do not speak in these ways because we believe that plants and inanimate objects cannot intentionally control their movements, and if they cannot control their movements they cannot be held responsible and morally evaluated. And if it turned out that there was no morally relevant difference between human actions and the movements of plants and inanimate objects, then human beings should not be held morally responsible either. For persons to be held morally responsible for their actions, there must be the kind of difference between actions and mere movements which justifies the application of moral concepts to the one but not the other. So here we have another reason for investigating the difference between the intentional and the nonintentional.

For our purposes it will be convenient to limit our discussion of intentional actions to those which necessarily involve *physical movement,* e.g., jumping out of a window. We will not consider those actions which might be said to be mental, such as conjuring up an image, searching one's memory for a name, or directing one's thoughts toward some philosophical problem, actions which might be said not to involve physical movement necessarily. We limit our discussions to bodily actions because we believe them to be the most important for determining the relation of mind and body, the thorniest problem in the philosophy of mind; we also believe them to be the most important for moral philosophy, since it is these actions which have most direct effect on others.

Furthermore, we will limit our discussion to those movements which are *intentional.* Many of the things we do, we do inadvertently, unknowingly, accidentally, by luck, or as a reflex. The very same action may be intentional under one description and not under another. For example, when I raise my arm, I may intentionally attract your attention and unintentionally rip my jacket. Throughout this chapter, when we speak of actions we will be thinking of intentional movements. Our task is to determine what makes such movements intentional.

Some theories of actions   To provide focus, let us use Wittgenstein's now classic formulation: "And the problem arises: what is left over if I subtract the fact that my arm goes up from the fact that I raise my arm?" (*Philosophical Investigations,* sec. 621.) What is the difference between a physical movement of my arm and my intentional action of moving my arm?

We will examine five theories of contemporary interest. (1) There is the view that intentional actions are those movements which are caused by particular sorts of mental events or states. On this view, what distinguishes my raising my arm is the kind of event or state preceding and causing the movement. What kind of event? Typically, on this theory, having certain reasons or making a decision, choice, or resolve to do the act. (2) On the theory of agency, the cause of the movement is not an event, rather, simply *the agent himself.* When I act, it is simply *I* who cause the movement. (3) A performative theory is that to say a movement is an intentional action is not to describe or report how things are or what caused what; it is to perform the act of assigning *responsibility* to an agent for the movement. (4) Some philosophers hold that the peculiar feature which makes a movement an action is that the movement is to be explained by citing a *goal* rather than some pre-existing cause such as a state, event, or agent. Finally, (5) there are contextual accounts of action, in which the crucial thing about holding that a movement is intentional is claimed to be that the movement is thereby conceived or described in a context of rules, norms, or practices.

Before considering these theories, it should be pointed out that they concern what makes an action *intentional* rather than what makes an action *voluntary*. These concepts are by no means the same. Examples of the one are not necessarily examples of the other. A long-time drug addict may take a shot of heroin intentionally, but he may take it against his will and not voluntarily; similarly, a prisoner under torture may intentionally tell where the guns are hidden, but he may not do so voluntarily. On the other hand, some voluntary acts may not be intentional. If you are showing me the sights, and, without telling me, take me off to Independence Hall, I may go voluntarily but not intentionally.

After examining these theories of intentional action, we shall consider their implications for the problem of voluntary action.

(1) Mental events as the causes of actions
The first theory to be considered has had many supporters since its advocacy by Descartes in the seventeenth century, although it has recently gone out of favor. It is the theory that "what is left over if I subtract the fact that my arm goes up from the fact that I raise my arm" is the occurrence of a mental event which is prior to my arm's going up and which causes it. What sort of mental cause? It may be the intention, decision, choice, resolve, or determination to raise my arm or having certain reasons for raising my arm.

Consider the following example: The teacher asks a question of the class and I, after deliberating, decide to raise my arm, and then do in fact raise it. On this theory, the deliberating produced an effect, the decision to raise my arm. That decision is then the cause, or, more accurately, a part of the cause of my arm's going up. It is only *part* of the cause, since other factors are also necessary for my arm to go up; I might decide to raise my arm but still my arm might fail to go up, because it is paralyzed, or I am suddenly struck dead by lightning, or I change my mind, or someone grabs my arm and holds it down. It is a *cause* in that it is the event which preceeds the arm's going up and which in those circumstances of my arm's not being paralyzed, etc., is sufficient for my arm's going up; given the decision, my arm must go up and without the decision it would not have gone up. (See pages 62-63, where the concept of cause is discussed.)

We have here a theory couched in traditional interactionist terms. The decision to raise the arm is a mental event and its causal consequence, the arm's going up, is the effect of that mental event. As so presented, the theory is clearly incompatible with epiphenomenalism and parallelism, theories which hold that mental events are never causes of physical events. If either of these two theories is true, than it is simply a factual mistake to think that my deciding to raise my arm had any part in causing my arm to go up; the truth of the matter would be that my deciding to raise my arm was itself a mere by-product or else a mere concomitant of brain events which caused both my deciding and also caused the arm to go up.

It should be noted, however, that this theory is compatible with certain forms of materialism, namely, behaviorism and the identity theory. On the former theory, mental events are to be analyzed dispositionally; in particular, deciding to raise one's arm might be construed as *becoming disposed* to raise one's arm. And acquiring such a disposition might well be part of the cause of one's arm going up. On the identity theory, mental events such as deciding to raise one's arm are identical with *brain events*. And such brain events might also well be part of the cause of one's arm going up. So despite the interactionist cast of this theory of action, given an appropriate account of mentalistic terms it is compatible with some forms of materialism. However, it is primarily in its dualistic setting, where mental events are taken to be different from physical events, that the theory is a matter of contemporary controversy.

In this dualistic setting, the theory that intentional actions have mental causes has come up against serious criticism. The attack begins with the observation that there are enormous numbers of cases in which an intentional action occurs but without any noticeable preceding conscious mental episode of intending, choosing, deciding, resolving, or determining. Such actions as striking the typewriter keys, moving one's legs in walking, turning a page as one reads, scratching an itch, turning one's head to watch a girl pass by, and giving someone a light are usually done without prior decision-making or deliberate choosing. We simply do these things straight away, as a matter of course. The absence of a conscious choice or deliberate decision does not mean that we do them as if in a coma, under hypnosis, by reflex, or involuntarily. We may do such actions intentionally, but without the preliminaries of conscious choice or decision.

To save the mental cause theory, some philosophers have introduced the notion of an *act of will* or *volition* which is supposed to precede and cause every action. Even when the volition is not what would be recognized as a conscious decision or deliberate choice, it still occurs and causes the movement. An action, then, is to be analyzed as a moment caused by a volition.

The doctrine of volitions, like the mind-body dualism which is its natural home, has been subjected to sustained and energetic criticism in the last few decades. Gilbert Ryle has led the way, denouncing the doctrine as a philosopher's myth, "an inevitable extension of the myth of the ghost in the machine." [2] Ryle presents the following objections to the doctrine. (1) There are no empirical grounds for thinking that *every* intentional action is preceded by a volition; in large numbers of cases of actions, no volition can be detected, despite the fact that according to the doctrine itself volitions are events of which we certainly should be aware if they did occur. (2) If the doctrine were true, one could at best only *infer* that any particular movement was done intentionally. In the case of other people, one could at best only infer the existence of the inner, private volition from their behavior; and, in one's own case, since causes can be known only by inductive inference, one could only infer inductively that the volition was indeed the *cause* of one's movement. But one can often know without inference, especially in one's own case, that a movement was done voluntarily. So the doctrine cannot be true. (3) We may ask of "volitions" whether they need prior volitions in order to occur. If so, than we are faced with an infinite regress of volitions; in order for a movement to occur intentionally, there must be a prior volition, but that volition requires a prior volition in order to occur itself, and so on, ad infinitum, making it impossible for *any* of them to occur. And if "volitions," which are, on the doctrine, *acts* of willing, do not need prior volitions in order to occupy, why should one think actions must have prior volitions?

Finally there is the objection that the appeal to causes here is a sham. [3] We are invited to consider the following famous analogy.

[2] Gilbert Ryle, *The Concept of Mind* (New York: Barnes & Noble, Inc., 1949), p. 63. His objections are to be found in Chapter III, section (2) of that book.

[3] One place where this is argued at length is in A. I. Melden, *Free Action* (New York: Humanities Press, Inc., 1961), Chapter 5.

When asked for the cause of a drug's putting someone to sleep, it might be replied that the cause is the drug's *soporific* power. Now this would be no explanation at all but only the appearance of an explanation, since "soporific" power means only "power to cause sleep." Thus we have said merely that the cause of the drug's putting someone to sleep is its property of causing people to go to sleep. We have "explained" the event by saying it was caused by that characteristic which causes such events. And that is not to say anything informative at all. It is suggested that we have the same situation if we claim that the cause of actions is some prior "volition"—for when we ask *what* a "volition" is, all we can say is that it is that prior mental event which causes the action. This becomes particularly evident if we focus our attention on those cases where we act without prior choosing or decision-making, those cases in which we simply face a particular situation and respond straight off and immediately. In such cases we are not aware of any conscious event which might be said to be the cause of the action. Hence the "volition" here can be understood only as "the cause of the action." We "explain" the action by saying it was caused by what causes such an action. In such a case no informative causal explanation is given, and hence the appeal to *causes* is a sham.

Now what exactly do these objections show? Ryle's first objection shows that volitions cannot be, in every instance, *conscious episodes*. But this does not rule out that they may sometimes be of a different nature; perhaps, when we have an action without conscious choice, the "volition" is the acquiring of a readiness to act under appropriate circumstances, i.e., a dispositional state. Ryle's second objection, that one could at best only *infer* the existence of volitions in others, assumes that one can have noninferential knowledge that another's action was intentional, a dubious assumption to say the least. We must postpone for later (see pp. 101-3, below) his assumption that one can have noninferential knowledge in one's own case. Ryle's third objection shows that either one must not conceive a volition to be itself an act (and one does not have to think of acquiring a disposition as an act) or one must not require that *every* act have a prior volition (one can think of volitions as mental acts which do not require a prior volition). And, finally, Melden's objection shows that for a volition to be causally explanatory, it must have more packed into it than merely being the cause of a particular action. If we take it to be a readiness to act (either a disposition or an identifiable experience of deciding) which need not result in action, then we can escape Melden's charge of vacuousness.

In short, it may well be that not every theory of actions as having mental causes will be refuted by these objections. We will postpone further consideration of the theory until we look more closely at whether actions can have causes at all.

(2) The theory of agency

One view which has recently appeared (although there are traces of it in Aristotle) is that in action, the cause of the movement is simply *the agent himself*. [4] An agent has the power to affect the world by producing actions. When it is said that the cause is the *agent himself*, it is meant that it should be ruled out that the cause is some *event*, even an event within the agent. The cause of actions is not an event but a *thing*, and such things, with the power to cause actions, are agents. Agent theorists would admit that large numbers of movements in the world are produced by prior events, but they would insist that some movements (for example, those constituting human actions) are not produced by prior events but by things (for example, men). And when a man causes an action, it is not some internal event or state of the man which causes the action; that would be the theory of mental events as the causes of actions. It is the man himself who, without undergoing any change himself, causes the action. Here, it is claimed, we have a basic and unique causal phenomenon not found in inanimate nature.

Theorists of this persuasion would admit that we sometimes talk as if inanimate objects were agents. We say that the *brick* broke the window and that the *rocket* rose from the launch pad into the skies. But they would hold that in such cases what we really mean is that some event which happened to the brick (e.g., its being hurled) caused the window to break or some *event* which happened to the rocket (e.g., the internal ignition of its fuel) caused it to rise. The brick or the rocket did not initiate the action or the set of events which led to the action. Even in the case of the rocket, where the lift-off was caused by internal events, those events themselves were not initiated by the rocket but by other events in the control tower outside the rocket. So that in these cases, although we talk as if the things were agents which acted, we do not really have actions caused by agents, but events caused by prior events. But, it would be

[4] This theory is sketched by Richard Taylor in *Metaphysics*, a companion volume in the Prentice-Hall Foundations of Philosophy Series, pp. 50-53, and defended at length in his *Action and Purpose* (Englewood Cliffs, N.J.: Prentice-Hall, Inc., 1966), especially Chapter 8. It is also presented by Roderick M. Chisholm in *Human Freedom and the Self* (Lawrence, Kansas: University of Kansas Press, 1964); pertinent parts are reprinted as "Freedom and Action," Part I, in *Freedom and Determinism*, ed. Keith Lehrer (New York: Random House, 1966).

argued, in the case of human actions we have the fundamentally different case of movements which are initiated by the men themselves. And that is to say we have the case of agents who cause movements without themselves undergoing any changes which are casually responsible for the movements.

It should be noted that one important motive for holding the theory of agency is to leave room for moral responsibility. Some defenders of this theory [5] maintain that if a movement has no cause, then the man who moves is not responsible for it, and if the movement is caused by events which themselves were not caused by the man, and hence were not under his control, then again he is not responsible for the movement. We shall look in more detail later (see pp. 106-10, below) at the question of moral responsibility and its relation to intentional action.

In assessing the theory of agency, we must note that it introduces a very different notion of causality from that which appears in the mental cause theory and, indeed, in epiphenomenalism and interactionism, as we have discussed them. On the latter theory, a cause is an *event* or *state* which is correlated with some subsequent event or state (namely, the effect) by a *law* so that we can appeal to the prior event or state to *predict* or *explain* the subsequent one; let us call this event-causation. The notion of causality in the theory of agency, let us call it agent-causation, lacks many of the important features of event-causation. For example, we do not have an *explanation* of the movement if all we know is that it was caused by an agent. Furthermore, we have no grounds for *prediction* of any particular effect if all we know is that an agent was acting or *prediction* of any particular kind of agent if all we know is that some particular effect was produced by an agent. Nor could there be any causal *laws* correlating kinds of causes and kinds of effects; and once we begin specifying kinds of agents, e.g., stingy men, we are moving toward a theory that it was his stinginess that caused the movement— and that is to move away from the theory of agency. In sum, it would appear that we no longer have the possibility of prediction, explanation, or causal laws, and hence no causal theory at all.

But even if we could admit that we have here an intelligible notion of causality (agency theorists would claim it is the most basic notion of cause), we need further argument to show that if a movement is caused by an agent then it *cannot* have a mental cause. For the considerations in the paragraph above show that if the theory of agency is a causal theory, it is causal in a very special

[5] Chisholm, *ibid.*, pp. 11-17.

sense of that word. So a movement which is agent-caused may also, in the event-cause sense, be caused by mental events.

Since agency theorists do seem to believe that agent-causation is incompatible with event-causation, let us look at the underlying picture which leads them to this belief. They think that if the action is caused by some prior (mental) event which is not identical with the agent, then the agent himself *plays no role* in producing and performing the action, so that the action would have occurred even if there were no agent at all! After all, if the prior (mental) event, not the agent, is sufficient to produce the action, then the agent is not necessary.[6] But this is absurd. It would be like arguing that since it is the sun's *emission of light rays* that causes us to tan, the sun itself plays no role in tanning us; or that since it is the motor's *turning of the drive shaft* that causes the car to move, the motor itself plays no role in making the car move. The sun in the one case and the motor in the other, rather than playing no role, are absolutely essential for the production of the effect. Of course, *some other agent* might have emitted the light rays or turned the drive shaft, but then it would be *that* agent which plays the crucial role in producing the effect. Similarly, in the case of actions, the prior (mental) events which are alleged to cause actions are events which happen to an *agent*. If there were no agent, there would be no such events and hence no such actions. So the agent does play a crucial role in producing the actions, even if the action is produced by some event in the agent.

The best way to think of the theory of agency is not with reference to the question "*Why* was action A performed?" but with reference to the question "*Who* performed action A?" Not that such questions are unimportant; they may well figure as a necessary *preliminary* to answering the question "Why?" Consider examples from inanimate nature. When we say that it is the *sun* which tans our skins, or it is the *motor* which makes the car move, we have not yet answered the question, "Why does our skin tan?" or "Why does the car move?" But we now know where to look for answers. Something about the sun or something about the motor will provide the answer to the question. Similarly, when we know *who* did the action, we know where to look for the answer to the question "Why was the action done?" So, far from being incompatible with the theory

6 Taylor expresses this thought as follows: "When I believe that I have done something, I do believe that it was I who caused it to be done, I who made something happen, and not merely something within me, such as one of my own subjective states, which is not identical with myself." (*Metaphysics*, pp. 50-51.)

that mental events cause actions, the theory of agency may well be a necessary supplement to it.

Furthermore, for moral purposes, for purposes of assigning responsibility, giving approval or disapproval, rewarding or punishing, and trying to make the world better by encouraging or discouraging certain actions, it is crucially important to call attention to the *agent* who did the action. And the agency theory does give a prominent place to this important element. However, it does so at the expense of omitting other important elements in our concept of intentional actions.

(3) A performative theory   Often we use words to assert some fact or give some information. But often we do something quite different with words. Suppose I say to you "I apologize." Despite the grammatical appearances, I am not primarily giving you a piece of information about myself; I am engaging in a social ritual the point of which is to publicly express my regret for some action of mine. To say "I apologize" is not to describe anything, or even say something which admits of truth or falsity; it is to perform an act, namely the act of apologizing. We have here an instance of what J. L. Austin named a performative utterance,[7] in which we use words not to describe what is the case but to perform a particular act. There are an enormous number of such uses of language, a few of which are "I name this ship the *Liberty*," "I warn you," "I do thee wed," "I promise," "I give you my marbles," "I second the motion," "I beg you to go home," "I give you my permission," "I find you guilty as charged," "I thank you," "I question that," and "I protest." In uttering these expressions in suitable circumstances, a person performs the act of naming a ship, warning someone, marrying, promising, making a gift, etc.

There has been great interest in recent times in the theory of performative utterances. It is a fascinating notion on its own, and has important applications for linguistics. But it has also been used in attempting to deal with traditional philosophical problems concerning the nature of knowledge, truth, and morality. Austin himself first presented the theory in connection with some problems in the theory of knowledge, suggesting that "I know" is not used to make a report about one's psychological state but is in important respects like such performatives as "I guarantee," "I give you my word," or

[7] J. L. Austin, "Performative Utterances," in the collection *J. L. Austin: Philosophical Papers*, ed. J. O. Urmson and G. J. Warnock (New York: Oxford University Press, 1961), pp. 220-39. A fuller treatment by Austin may be found in his *How to Do Things with Words*, ed. J. O. Urmson (New York: Oxford University Press, 1965).

"I stake my reputation." [8] Strawson has argued that to say of a proposition that it "is true" is not to make an assertion about the proposition but to perform the act of endorsing or accepting the proposition.[9] And in the field of ethics, it has been maintained that to say of something that it is *good* or *bad, right* or *wrong,* is not to describe the thing in question but to perform the act of *grading* it [10] or the act of commending or condemning it.[11] Our interest here, though, is in seeing how the theory of performative utterances can be applied to the problem of intentional action.

Consider the performative "I take full responsibility for that act." To utter it in appropriate circumstances is to perform the act of taking responsibility, an act by which I render myself liable for the consequences and open myself up to possible blame, recrimination, and punishment for the act. Similarly, to say "I hold you fully responsible for that act" is to perform the act of holding you liable for the consequences of that act.

A performative theory of intentional actions is a theory that to say "Jones did it *intentionally*" is not primarily to report something about Jones but primarily to perform the act of *assigning responsibility* or *liability* to Jones for the act.[12] And when I say of myself "I did it *intentionally*," then I perform the act of *taking responsibility* and *assuming liability* for what I did. Of course, such utterances also have a descriptive component, as is the case with many performatives. If I give you a warning, "I warn you that the police are on the way," I do describe the police as coming, and that is to give information, say something which admits of truth or falsity, but the "I warn you" component is purely performative. Similarly, "Jones did it—whether intentionally or not I do not say" is descriptive. "Jones did it *intentionally*" adds no further information to the previous statement, but it does add the performative element of holding

[8] J. L. Austin, "Other Minds," *Proceedings of the Aristotelian Society,* Suppl. Vol. XX (1946), reprinted in *Logic and Language,* Second Series, ed. Antony Flew (New York: Philosophical Library, 1953), and in *J. L. Austin: Philosophical Papers.*

[9] P. F. Strawson, "Truth," *Analysis,* IX, No. 6 (1949), reprinted in *Philosophy and Analysis,* ed. Margaret MacDonald (New York: Philosophical Library, 1955).

[10] J. O. Urmson, "On Grading," *Mind,* LIX (1950), 145-69, reprinted in *Language and Logic,* Second Series.

[11] R. M. Hare, *Language of Morals* (New York: Oxford University Press, 1952) and *Freedom and Reason* (New York: Oxford University Press, 1963).

[12] This theory is similar in some respects to one developed by H. L. A. Hart, "The Ascription of Responsibility and Rights," *Proceedings of the Aristotelian Society,* Vol. XLIX (1948-49), pp. 171-94, reprinted in *Logic and Language,* First Series, ed. Antony Flew (New York: Philosophical Library, 1952). Hart's theory is usually called ascriptivism.

Jones responsible for doing it. Thus, in giving an analysis of intentional actions, we do not have to look for any further descriptive element such as a prior mental cause or an agent-cause, as the theories discussed above would have it, nor a teleological cause or reference to norms as theories to be discussed below would have it.

Now there are a number of criticisms to be made of this theory. (1) It is not the case that everything we do intentionally is something we are to be held responsible or liable for. As was pointed out above (see page 81), we may do things intentionally but not voluntarily—for example, under extreme duress or provocation, or because of addiction, neurotic compulsion, or irresistible impulse—and in such cases we would not ordinarily be responsible or liable for what we did. So doing something intentionally is not a sufficient condition for being responsible for it. (2) It is an essential mark of the performative element in an utterance that it is neither true or false, since it does not state, assert, describe, or report. But the claim that someone did it intentionally does admit of truth or falsity, and is either true or false depending upon whether he did it intentionally or not. Given that some act occurred, one can believe that it was done *intentionally* and be mistaken (even about an act of one's own, e.g., one done years ago), and one can say the act was done intentionally and be lying; such things are not the case for bona fide performatives like "I congratulate you" or "I protest." (3) Doing something intentionally is at best a *necessary* condition for being responsible for doing it, but it is not a necessary condition for being *held* responsible; a person can be *held* responsible (even by himself) for something he did not do intentionally and therefore is not responsible for. Also he can be responsible for something and not be *held* responsible for it. The act of assigning or assuming responsibility can perfectly well occur or not occur quite independently of whether or not it is true that the act was done intentionally. For these three reasons it is implausible to claim that to say someone did something *intentionally* is identical with the act of assigning *responsibility* for the action to that person.

To be sure, there is a relation between assigning responsibility for an action and saying that the action was intentional. The relation would seem to be this, that when we assign responsibility for an act, we imply that we believe the person did the act intentionally; to say "I hold you [or myself] responsible for the act" while not believing the act was intentional is to be insincere. Believing the act was intentional is a presupposition of the sincere performance of assigning responsibility. But that is hardly to say they are identical.

It is undeniable that the attributions of responsibility and intentions are not purely descriptive; they do involve a performative element. In such cases we do not merely describe the world objectively and coldly. We also take a stand, render a verdict, and commit ourselves to practical consequences of praise and blame, punishment and reward, approval and disapproval. But it is clearly a mistake to think that no element of description is involved. When we hold a person responsible or say he did something intentionally, we allege that his action was done on purpose, done for a reason. And this is to say something about the agent's *frame of mind* when he did the action. Therefore, let us turn to the next theory, which does explicitly bring in the notion of purpose.

(4) Goals as the explanation of actions   It is characteristic of many actions that they are performed with some purpose in mind, with the intention of bringing about some state of affairs, aimed toward some goal. I do not merely move my hand; I reach for the grapes. I do not merely revise my will; I disinherit my spendthrift nephew. I do not merely sign my name; I enlist in the Peace Corps. The action is done for the sake of some future state of affairs which, it is hoped, will be brought about by the action.

The future state of affairs comes into the picture in two important ways. First, we refer to it to *explain* the action: "*Why* did he move his hand?" "To get the grapes." We understand the action in terms of the end state it was designed to achieve. Second, we often refer to it to *describe* the action. "*What* did he do?" "He reached for the the grapes." Here explaining and describing may well come to the same thing. Suppose I write my name. Am I signing a check, or am I practicing my handwriting, or am I testing a pen, or am I forging the signature of someone who happens to have the same name as mine, or am I trying to learn what my name is by observing what name I write down? Each of these may function both as a description and explanation of what action I am performing. What determines which, if any, of these explanatory descriptions is appropriate, is the future state at which I am aiming, i.e., what my *purpose* is when I write my name down.

An explanation which consists of a description in terms of the end, result, or goal aimed at is often called a teleological explanation. It would be the thesis of theorists of this persuasion that what makes a movement an intentional action is that it is appropriate to give a teleological explanation for that movement.[13]

---

[13] This view is defended by Charles Taylor in *The Explanation of Behavior* (New York: Humanities Press, 1964). See also Richard Taylor, *Action and Purpose*.

In favor of the teleological thesis, it can be pointed out that we do have here a kind of explanation especially appropriate to movements which are actions. For ordinary explanations of movements which are not actions—for example, why the eightball moved—no appeal to ends or goals or results is necessary or appropriate. It did not move in order to get into the side pocket; it moved simply because it was hit by another ball with a particular velocity. But of the pool player we can ask *why* he moved the eightball and expect an answer of the form *"in order to* get it into the side pocket." The appeal to ends or goals is necessary and appropriate to the explanation of movements which are actions. So far, there is little controversy about the teleological thesis.

Controversy arises when philosophers go on to claim that we have here a unique kind of explanation irreducibly different from and incompatible with ordinary *causal explanation in terms of prior circumstances*. It is this claim that we must examine.

There are three doctrines to be distinguished here. (1) There is the doctrine that it is the *future* event which brings about, produces, or prompts my present behavior; on this account, the primary difference between final causation and the ordinary sort of causation, sometimes called efficient causation, is that the cause is a future event rather than a past event. This view is obviously incompatible with the theory discussed above that actions are caused by *prior* (mental) events. (2) There is the more subtle doctrine that the cause of my present behavior is a rather peculiar feature of the *prior* circumstances, namely that in those circumstances just that behavior is *required* for the production of the future goal-state. It is the *requiredness* of the behavior which causes the behavior to occur.[14] (3) Finally there is the modest doctrine that in order fully to understand or *explain* the action, we must cite the future state aimed at. If we say the future state is the "cause" of the action, we are not using that term in the sense of "efficient cause" but in the sense of the point or rationale of the action. Let us examine each of these versions in more detail.

(1) Even if we allow, just for the sake of the argument, that a future event can causally effect a present event, we can still easily dispose of the first doctrine so far as the explanation of actions is concerned. It *cannot* be the case that every action is produced by the future goal-state toward which it aims for the simple reason that, in many cases at least, the future goal-state never obtains, is never achieved. My action may well be a genuine case of reaching for the

[14] This view is suggested by Charles Taylor, *The Explanation of Behavior*, Chapter 1.

grapes, but I may fail to get them; in such a case, *getting the grapes* cannot be the cause of my reaching for them because it never occurs and, therefore, cannot be the cause of anything.

(2) It is not very plausible to claim that the mere requiredness of the behavior is sufficient to produce it. There may be some truth in the proverb that necessity is the mother of invention, but mere necessity cannot of itself alone bring something into being. We know of too many tragic cases where an action required to achieve some goal-state never occurs. For example, the agent may not realize that the action is required. For the action to be forthcoming, at the very least he must *believe* that the production of the goal-state requires the action. And once this is pointed out it becomes obvious that it is not even necessary that the action *in fact* be required but only that it be (perhaps mistakenly) believed to be required. For example, if we ask why he stopped the car, "To get gas" may be a perfectly good explanation even if he does not realize that the gas station is closed and therefore the goal-state of getting gas does not require the action of his stopping there. But once we modify the doctrine so that it concerns the mental state of the agent, e.g., his beliefs and desires, it no longer is distinguishable from the earlier theory that prior mental circumstances are the causes of action.

(3) It is undeniable that we often explain actions in terms of the future state aimed at, so that knowing a person's goal may well be essential to understanding his action. Here we have a kind of explanation especially appropriate to human beings and higher animals ("Why is your cat bringing that bird in *here*?" "To let us know what a good hunter she is."). Where it has application to non-conscious things, it is either metaphorical ("Water *seeks* the lowest level"), derivative of the purposes of the designer ("The purpose of the battery is to allow the car to start"), or by analogy with a designed system ("The purpose of the heart is to keep the blood circulating").

We enter into the area of controversy when we ask if there is any *incompatibility* between explanation of action in terms of the intended goals and explanation by appeal to prior efficient causes. It would seem that there is not. For if we mention a *future* state which is aimed at, then we can refer to the *present* or *past state of aiming*, that is, the present or past intention to achieve that future state. So for every teleological explanation, there could be a parallel explanation in terms of the causal efficacy of the intention. It would take further argument, which we will examine later, to show that actions cannot be explained in terms of prior causes.

Another way to put this criticism of the teleological thesis is to say that the appropriateness of reason-explanations of movements which are actions does not force us to accept a special, unique, and irreducible *kind* of explanation. We may well simply have a special kind of state or event, namely the mental state of having certain sorts of reasons, goals, ends in view, which causes (in the familiar sense of prior efficient circumstances) the movement. The later option is still open to us.

(5) Contextual accounts of actions

The theory we must now examine holds that what is distinctive about actions is an implicit reference to *some set of rules, norms, practices, principles, or standards in terms of which the action is described and can be evaluated.* We shall call proponents of this view contextualists.[15]

Consider a move being made by a chess player. Someone ignorant of chess might observe merely that a particular piece of wood is transferred by hand from one location to another. But someone who knows chess would observe that a *player* has just *moved* his *knight.* Here we have an action described in terms of the rules of chess, which lay down what a *player* is, what a *knight* is, and what an allowable *move* is; the action-description itself involves reference to the rules of chess. Furthermore, there is also an implicit reference to evaluation. As an action in a chess game, it is a good, bad, or indifferent action in terms of goals which are also determined by the rules of the game. It is to be expected that the player had some *reason* for making the move; although an occasional move may be random, someone who always moved at random could hardly be said to be playing chess. And we can evaluate the player's reason as good, bad, or indifferent. What makes it a particular action, e.g,. *moving a knight,* is its conformity to the rules of chess and its liability to evaluation in terms of the standards of good chess.

Similar remarks could be made about other sorts of actions. "Signaling a left turn" is characterized and justified in terms of the rules of the road, "writing a will" in a legal and moral context. To describe an action as "preparing a dinner" is to make tacit reference to rules of etiquette, culinary principles, standards of health and taste, and principles of economy. "Giving your side of the argument" involves reference to rules of logic, scientific procedure, and rationality in general. Actions are typically done for reasons, and reasons involve reference to rules, standards, norms, and principles.

It cannot be denied that rules enter into the very description of

[15] For defense of such theories, see Melden, *Free Action,* and R. S. Peters, *The Concept of Motivation* (New York: Humanities Press, 1958).

large numbers of actions. But it will not do to appeal to this fact as bringing out the difference between actions and physical movements. For there are cases in which rules enter into the very description of physical movements as well. If I say that the ball landed in right field, terms like "ball" and "right field" clearly are rule-dependent; such a description makes sense only in the context of the rules of baseball. Yet clearly just a physical movement and not an action is involved here.

Might it not also be said that there are many simple actions, like *raising one's arm*, which do not depend upon a context of rules or norms? Well, a contextualist might reply that even a description like "raising one's arm" to some degree depends upon context. Suppose you are in a classroom and the teacher has just asked a question. At that point, your arm goes up, and let us suppose that *some* intentional action is performed. Is it beyond doubt that a proper description of the action intended is "You raised your arm"? Suppose you were reaching to catch a fly, or pointing to the clock to remind the teacher of the time, or just stretching, or lifting something up in your hand. Would it not be false to describe your action as raising your arm? Might it not well be the case that your arm's going up was *unintentional* even though you did intentionally reach to catch the fly? In that case, in the sense of "action" we have been using all along, which is short for doing something intentionally, "You raised your arm" would not be a correct description of your action.

But what is brought out by this case is not that the appropriateness of a description like "He raised his arm" is dependent upon a context of rules and norms but that the appropriateness of such a description is dependent upon the agent's *intention*. And this is even more obviously the case for those actions more complex than simply raising one's arm. As we have noted, a person who moved chess pieces randomly about could hardly be said to be playing chess, even if it luckily turned out that the moves were astonishingly brilliant.

This point can be brought out in another way. When it is a question of applying rules or norms in the description of an action, we must make sure that we apply the *appropriate* ones. And the appropriateness of the rules or norms will depend upon whether the agent intended to act in accordance with those rules or norms.

The problem, then, is to give an account of *intentions*. If they are mental states or events, then we have come back to the first theory we examined, in which actions are movements with mental causes. If the contextualist is to make out his case, he must give a contextual account of intentions.

Let us say that to act intentionally or intend to act some way is to be prepared to give *reasons* to *justify* the action. To give reasons is to show how things will be better for the action's having occurred. What one thinks of as "things being better" will, of course, depend upon what one wants; and the choice of the action will depend upon one's belief that the action will satisfy one's wants. So one's reasons may be poor reasons or good reasons insofar as the relevant wants and beliefs are reasonable or not. But what makes an action intentional, on this account, is that the agent is prepared to stand behind the action, to defend its propriety, by an appeal to facts and values which purport to justify the action. Not that a person would have to defend the action's propriety forever, since one might change one's mind about its propriety; but one would have to be prepared to defend its propriety when doing it or when intending to do it.

Such an account of intention would seem to give support to the contextualist's effort to provide a noncausal account, for it does seem that to give *justifying reasons* for an action is to do something very different from giving a *causal explanation* of the action. The latter involves citing prior events and empirical laws which correlate those events with subsequent events, whereas the former involves showing how the action is a case of how things *ought* to be. So it would seem that if we characterize intentional actions as those which the person is prepared to defend in the context of justification, then we can avoid characterizing them by their cause, as the other theories would have us do.

Unfortunately for the contextualist, this account will not do. For it is possible for something *unintentional* to happen which may still meet the appropriate norms, and it may even be the case that the person involved is prepared to defend the propriety of what happened in terms of those norms. For example, consider a chess player who has decided to make a move which he believes to be just the right move and for which he is prepared to give excellent reasons; but before he can make the move he suffers a sudden but short-lived paroxysm in the course of which his hand knocks the piece he had intended to move onto the exact square to which he had intended to move it. So the brilliant move is made, and he is prepared to defend the move, but still he did not make the move *intentionally*. A rather bizarre set of events, I admit, but still possible, and instructive. For what it shows is that it is not enough for one's action to be intentional that one have reasons for doing it. It must also be the case that one's reasons make a difference, that they *lead* one to do it, that one does it *for* those reasons, *be-*

cause of those reasons, and if all the circumstances had remained the same except that one did not have those reasons, then one would not have done it. One's reasons must be *operative*; they must do work.

When we say of a person that he is just "rationalizing" or giving just a "rationalization," we often mean that the reasons he gives for his action, sensible as they may be, were not his "real" reasons, were not the reasons he actually had which led him to do it. In this sense of "rationalization," we can put our most basic criticism of contextualism by saying that it cannot account for the distinction between a person's reasons and rationalizations.

Reasons and causes   We have found various difficulties with all of the leading theories. But there is more to be said for the mental-cause theory than we have so far considered, particularly in light of the final criticism we made of contextualism, namely that in intentional actions one's reasons must make a difference. If that is true, it looks suspiciously like saying that one's reasons must be causally efficacious.

The relation between *actions* and the wants and beliefs which constitute *reasons* for action is complicated by the intervening presence of "volitions" (see page 83, above). Sometimes actions are preceded by introspectably noticeable decisions, acts of choice, or formings of intention; sometimes they are preceded merely by the formation of dispositions to act appropriately under the proper conditions. If one holds that one's reasons *cause* one's actions, then when there is a decision or disposition to act, one would hold that one's reasons cause the decision or disposition which in turn causes the action. Although when we talk of the relation of reasons to decisions or dispositions we often say that one's reasons *led* one to decide this or be disposed to do that, we also often say what *made* a person decide this or be disposed to do that. If there are good reasons for saying that actions are *caused* by reasons, then the presence of decisions or dispositions does complicate the causal story by introducing a further link in the causal chain, but I do not see that it gives any further grounds for supporting or rejecting reasons as causes.

To give us a specific example with which to work, let us suppose I suddenly put my head down between my legs. Later on, you ask me why I did that, and I reply "Because I felt faint." Here I give you my reason for an intentional action. Actually, as is usually the case when we give reasons, I give only a part of my reason—the rest is too obvious. But suppose you don't see any connection and say "So?" I reply "Well, I believed I was about to faint, I wanted to prevent myself from fainting, and it is my understanding that putting one's head between one's legs prevents fainting." I cite the *beliefs* and *wants* I had when I made that movement. But why do I pick *these* out? Surely I had other wants at the time (perhaps I also wanted to go home; but that is not why I put my head down) and other beliefs as well. What is it to cite *these* wants and beliefs as my "reasons" for acting?

To cite my *reasons* for acting is to cite those beliefs and wants which were the *telling* ones, which were responsible for my so acting, which were such that I would not have acted that way if I had not had them at that time. Do we not have here a relationship most naturally classified as a *causal* relationship between these wants and beliefs on the one hand and my action on the other?

It would seem, in light of the foregoing considerations, that one's reasons for doing something (as contrasted with the rationalizations one might give) must be causally efficacious in producing the action. However, many contemporary philosophers resist this conclusion. They maintain that reasons are not causes, on the grounds that the relation between reasons and action is very different from the relation between cause and effect. We shall examine three purported differences between reasons–action and cause–effect: (1) that cause and effect must be logically independent of each other, whereas reasons and actions are not; (2) that cause–effect relationships must be instances of generalizations, whereas reason–action relationships are not; and (3) that causal relationships can be known only on the basis of inductive evidence, whereas one can know the reasons for one's own action without such evidence.[16]

(1) It is frequently said that causes and their effects must be logically independent of each other in such a way that the existence or nonexistence of the one must in no way logically entail the existence or nonexistence of the other. It is often claimed, however, that the reasons for an action are not logically independent of the action.[17] This claim is based upon the indisputable fact that the very description of the reasons for acting a particular way must make mention of the action, since the reasons are, of necessity, the reasons to do such-and-such. Thus the alleged cause gets its very characterization from the nature of the alleged effect. From this it is concluded

---

[16] For fuller discussion of these and other attempts, see the article, to which I am much indebted, by Donald Davidson, "Actions, Reasons, and Causes," *The Journal of Philosophy*, LX, No. 23 (1963), 685-700, especially pp. 693-700.

[17] See Melden, *Free Action*, Chapter 12. The same principle is used by Melden in the argument, cited above (pp. 83-84), against the concept of volitions.

that reasons and actions are not logically independent, and, therefore, cannot be causally connected.

It might be replied that there are many ordinary cases of cause and effect in which the descriptions are not logically independent. "Suntans are caused by the sun" is such a case; here the effect is characterized by the cause. In "Tuberculosis is caused by the tubercle bacillus," the cause is characterized by its effect. Yet in both cases we have a genuine causal relationship.

However, a problem still remains, for, to take the case of "Suntans are caused by the sun," we can replace "suntans" by *another description*, e.g., "nonartificially induced tans," which will allow us to assert that causal relationship without mentioning the cause. In general, when two kinds of events are causally connected, we can find some description of them which brings out the significant causal relationship without begging any questions.

But in the case of reasons, the description of the action to be performed *must* figure in the statement of the reasons, or else they would not be reasons for doing *that*. Of course, in any particular case, we can sometimes pick out those reasons by a description which makes no mention of the action (e.g., the reasons he considered from 1 P.M. to 1:15 P.M.), but there is no guarantee that we will always be able to do so. Furthermore, if we did that, we would no longer have an *explanation* of the action.

Despite the fact that we may not be able to refer to those reasons without mentioning the action, the objection still fails. For when the action is mentioned in characterizing the reasons, there is no implication that the action will occur. I may have the best reasons in the world to do something and yet the action may still not occur because, for example, I am prevented from doing it. And if the action does occur, there is no implication that it was done for those or some other particular set of reasons. Consider the expectation of a rising stock market. To describe this expectation, we must mention the rising stock market. But that does not imply that the market will rise, nor does a rising market imply any expectations about it. So the expectation of a rising market and a rising market are logically independent in that the existence or nonexistence of the one in no way entails the existence or nonexistence of the other. Hence there is nothing to bar the existence of a causal connection between the two. And as is known, there is indeed a causal connection between them.

Similarly, the existence of my reasons for doing some action in no way entails that the action will occur and vice versa. Like "expectation of," "reason for" is an "intentional" notion (see page 23), containing internal reference to something, but it is logically independent of what it refers to, and can therefore be causally connected with what it refers to.

Since one's reasons typically consist of one's *beliefs* and *wants* at the time, it should be pointed out that these too are logically independent of actions. That I *believe* I am about to faint and that putting my head between my legs will prevent fainting in no way entails that I will put my head between my legs, or vice versa. Similarly that I *want* to prevent myself from fainting in no way entails that I will put my head between my legs. Nor do the beliefs and wants jointly necessitate any action. Nor would any other beliefs or wants we might add necessitate any action.

Some philosophers hold that there are very *general* necessary statements connecting reasons and movements. They hold that it could not be the case that reasons *never* lead to movements; it could not be the case that even though people had the best of reasons for doing something, no reason not to, and nothing to prevent them from doing it, still they never did it. But I would disagree. Consider the desire to kill oneself—many people have reason and opportunity but just don't.

Of course, there are some descriptions of action which do logically entail the existence of certain reasons. If I go to the store for bread, then my reason is to get bread. Admittedly it would be odd to speak of cause and effect here. But if we subtract the reason (viz., for bread) from the description of the action, then there is no oddness in speaking of cause and effect. That I went to the store does not even entail that I wanted to go to the store—I might have wanted to go to a bar and mistook the store for a bar.

(2) Usually when we have a causal explanation of an event by some prior circumstances, we appeal either explicitly or implicitly to a *generalization* which links cause and effect by stating that whenever the prior circumstances obtain the event follows. It is clear that reasons and action do not meet this condition. I would not *always* put my head down between my legs if I felt faint; e.g., if I were on the drill field. Some philosophers conclude from this that we do not have a causal connection here.[18]

In reply, two remarks should be made. First, even in cases of indisputable *causal* connections, we often cannot cite a plausible generalization. If a window breaks when struck by a rock, are we

[18] H. L. A. Hart and A. M. Honoré, *Causation in the Law* (New York: Oxford University Press, 1959), p. 52.

always in a position to say that whenever a window of that type is struck by a rock of that size moving at that velocity the window will break? Even when we cannot cite any specific generalization, do we have the slightest doubt that the rock's striking the window was the cause of the window's breaking? If we are willing to accept a causal connection without being able to cite a law in the case of the rock's causing the window to break, we should not reject a causal connection in the case of reasons and action just because no generalization is at hand there.

Second, although there is no *simple* law connecting reasons and actions, there may well be complex laws which *include* them. Surely part of my reason for putting my head between my legs when I do is that I believe I am not on the drill field and therefore I believe my action will not have the adverse effects it would if I were on the drill field. When I cite my reasons for acting, I only give part of the story; if I were to give the whole story, then we might indeed have something which would support a lawful generalization.

Such a generalization would be of the form: Whenever a person has such-and-such wants and beliefs and is in such-and-such circumstances (the latter is needed because a person may be prevented from acting by his circumstances even if he has all the reason in the world to so act), then he will act in such-and-such a way. Even a generalization of that form might not be true of all men all the time. Perhaps it is only true of *rational* men or of men when they are rational. To make it true in all cases we might have to add a further description of the kind of person to which the law applies. But there does not seem to be any feature here which is not paralleled in cases of ordinary causal relationships.

(3) Another important feature of ordinary causal relationships seems to be lacking in the case of reasons and actions. In the ordinary cases, to know that A is the *cause* of B rather than a mere accidental predecessor of B, one must have *evidence*, and this evidence must be in the form of experience of analogous cases, or, in complex cases, in the form of more elaborate kinds of inferential reasoning. But it would seem that in a good many of the cases in which an agent acts for a particular reason, that agent can know what his reason was without the need of experience of analogous cases or of other kinds of inferential reasoning. For example, the first time one sees lightning and then hears thunder, one cannot be said to *know* that the lightning caused the thunder, for there are many other things which preceded the thunder which might have been the cause. It is only after many experiences of lightning followed by

thunder, plus perhaps some further theoretical information, that one can be said to know that the lightning caused the thunder. But it would seem that in a good many cases in which an agent acts for a particular reason, the agent can know what his reason for acting that way was without the need of experience of analogous cases or of more theoretical information. I can know that I put my head between my legs because I felt faint without having to appeal to other cases in which feeling faint was followed by putting one's head between one's legs. There may well have been many other wants and beliefs which I had during the time before I put my head down, but I know, without further experience, that my reason for acting that way was to avoid fainting. And I may know this even if it is the very first time in my life that I ever felt faint and put my head down. It would be absurd to claim that I *infer* the causal connection from general knowledge about how people who feel faint behave or about what events precede the act of putting one's head between one's legs. I just know, without appeal to such information, why I acted that way. Of course someone else observing my behavior might know why I put my head down, but he would have to appeal to further information about me or about people in general to arrive at and justify this knowledge.

If we do indeed have a factor here that is missing in cases of ordinary causal relationships, there are two possible conclusions to be drawn. One is that we do not have a causal relationship at all between reasons and actions. The other is that we have an extraordinary causal relationship, sometimes referred to as a non-Humean cause. On this view, there is in such cases a necessary connection between cause and effect which can be known in the individual case without appeal to similar cases.

It is my own view that the relation of reasons to action is a case of the ordinary kind of causal relationship. Yet it is true that often, when one gives one's reasons there is no question of providing *evidence*. How is this to be explained?

I believe that part of the explanation comes from the fact, noted above (see page 25), that many of a person's own mental states are private to him. Others have to observe his behavior to know his wants and beliefs, but he can know *without observation* what were his beliefs and wants prior to acting—and this includes the degree of intensity of his wants and the degree of conviction of his beliefs. That gives him a great advantage over others so far as giving the reasons for his action is concerned. Others must first determine on the basis of evidence what his frame of mind was. Here we have one source of the fact that the agent does not need to appeal to *evidence* in giving his reasons for the action.

If we eliminate this factor, by considering only those cases in which others know as much about one's prior frame of mind as one does oneself, is there still a "noninductive" element in the determination of the reasons? There still does seem to be, in that one does not usually arrive at the judgment of reasons by inductive reasoning. One can simply say, straight off, what one's reasons were. And it should be noted that *others*, if they knew one's frame of mind, would usually also say, straight off, what one's reasons were; there is no privileged access here, once the frame of mind is publicly known.

But this is a mere matter of psychology. We often determine straight off and without reasoning what caused what, in ordinary cases of physical interactions as well as in mental interactions. How we arrive at our judgments is not relevant here. What is relevant is how the judgments are to be justified. And when we raise this question, it can be seen that there is no special "noninductive" element so far as stating one's reasons for acting is concerned. This is shown by the fact that when a person cites his reasons for acting, he may be sincere in believing that those were his reasons and yet *he may still be mistaken*. A person may believe that he put his head between his legs because he felt faint, but this may not be the true reason. He may really have wished to call attention to himself or ruin the parade. These may have been the real factors at work, although he may not realize this. It is a notorious fact that people often deceive themselves about their own reasons for acting.

How do we show that a particular belief about the reasons for acting is erroneous? By pointing to similar cases. We may cite other instances in which his wish to call attention to himself was followed by bizarre behavior. By citing other instances we do not cast doubt on his claim that he felt faint but on his claim that he put his head down *because* he felt faint. And in proceeding in this way we are treating purported reasons for action in exactly the same way we treat purported causes; we subject them to the test of analogous instances. Thus this apparent difference between reasons and causes drops away.

Even if we may have failed to put our finger on any specific differences between cause–effect and reason–action, the feeling may linger that they are still quite different. There are a number of possible sources of this feeling, all of them, I believe, involving confusion. We have already noticed one when we looked at the theory of agency (see page 87, above). The idea was expressed there that if actions have causes other than agents (and one's reasons are not themselves an agent), then actions cannot be *done* by agents, as though if one's reasons caused the action then one's reasons must have *done* the action. There is another source of confusion possible, namely that if actions are *effects* of anything, then they merely *happen* to persons, who are thereby rendered passive and "helpless victims" [19] of the events which befall them rather than active agents doing things on their own. But why should one believe that? If my action is the effect of my own hard thinking about the best way to satisfy my own need, then in no sense am I a "helpless victim."

Finally, there is the source of confusion which comes from taking too narrow a view of causality. It is sometimes said that to construe reasons as causes of action is to construe them as "para-mechanical thrusts" from a ghostly engine or as invisible levers and pulleys from machinery off stage. But to say that one thing causes another is not to say what kind of cause it is, and it certainly is not to say it is the kind of *mechanical* cause described in nineteenth century physics books. Reasons can be causes of actions without being mechanical causes; even in physics such causes are no longer thought to be the only sorts that exist. Our reasons can move us even if they do not do so in the way that one billiard ball moves another or the moon moves the tides.

The mental cause theory revisited

If we have removed the various objections to holding that reasons can be causes of action, then it becomes appropriate to re-examine the mental cause theory, that the difference between an intentional action like my raising my arm and my arm's going up when I do not raise it intentionally is that the intentional action is caused by a prior mental event or state. Now if we specify the theory further by adding that the mental event or state is to be some set of wants and beliefs, the sorts of things that go to constitute reasons, then we have the theory that intentional actions are those occurrences which have reasons as causes.

There are two lines of attack against this theory: (1) that reason-causes are not necessary for actions to be intentional, and (2) that reason-causes are not sufficient for actions to be intentional.

(1) It might be claimed that it is not necessary that there always be a reason for everything we do intentionally. If I pick a piece of lint from my sleeve, do I have *a reason*? The reply to this is that when we speak of reasons here, we do not necessarily mean deep, profound, or surprising reasons. A person may take a piece of lint

[19] See Melden, *Free Action*, pp. 7, 129.

from his sleeve simply because *he wants to* or because *he feels like doing it.* One's reasons can be very simple, and often are. If we understand "reasons" in this way, then it is the case that we always have a reason for what we do intentionally, for whatever we do intentionally we either just want to do or else have more elaborate reasons for doing. So having a reason-cause is a necessary condition of acting intentionally.

(2) It might be claimed that having a reason as a cause is not sufficient for an action to be intentional. This objection must be distinguished from the more easily disposable one that reasons are not sufficient conditions of action in the sense that even with the best of reasons the action may not occur (because it is prevented, for example). The latter objection is not to the point because the mental cause theory is only meant to apply to those cases in which the action does in fact occur; for those cases, the theory holds that what makes the action *intentional* is the prior occurrence of a reason-cause of the action. The former, more serious objection is that even where the action does occur, it may have a reason as its cause and still not be an intentional action, so that having a reason-cause is not sufficient for making an action *intentional.*

The following example can be offered to support this objection.[20] A man wants to inherit a fortune and believes that he will do so if he kills his uncle. Let us say he decides to kill his uncle. This decision throws him into such a state of agitation that, while driving, he begins speeding and accidentally hits another car, killing a passenger who turns out to be his very uncle. Here we have a case of a man with reasons to kill his uncle, and whose reasons cause him to kill his uncle, but who nevertheless did not kill his uncle intentionally (although it might be hard to convince a jury of that).

What further condition must we add to take account of such a case? It is a case in which the end (the death of the uncle) requires a means. The fortunate nephew intends the end but does not intend the means (crashing into the car which contains his uncle). To deal with this, we must add the further condition that where it is necessary to employ some means in achieving an end, to bring about the end intentionally one must also bring about the means intentionally. Thus the nephew must *intentionally* crash into his uncle's car. On the mental cause theory here advocated, he must have reasons for doing it (e.g., he wants to) and his wanting to do it must cause it to happen. Since the nephew did not want to crash into the car, he

[20] A basically similar example is given by Roderick M. Chisholm in his essay, "Freedom and Action," in *Freedom and Determinism,* ed. Lehrer, p. 30.

did not do it intentionally and, therefore, did not intentionally kill his uncle. So the purported counterexample fails.

Let us now summarize the mental cause theory. In the simplest case, I make some movement, A, intentionally if and only if I want A to occur and that want causes A to occur. Where a volition (e.g., a decision) intervenes, then the want causes the volition which causes the occurrence. In the more complex cases where the occurrence of A is a means toward the occurence of B, if I want B to occur and I believe that A will produce B, and the want and the belief (i.e., my reasons) cause A to occur, then and only then does A occur intentionally. For even more complex cases the account would have to be appropriately more complicated, but I believe that an account along these lines is the most plausible way of analyzing what makes an action *intentional*.

The problem of free will

We have been examining the view that reasons are causes of our decisions and our actions. One great source of resistance to this view is the idea that it commits us to denying that there are any *voluntary* actions, actions done of the agent's own *free will*. That idea comes about in the following way. Suppose one asks *"What causes the wants and beliefs* that constitute reasons?" There are two possibilities. Either (1) the wants and beliefs themselves have no causes, arising spontaneously and randomly, or else (2) they themselves are caused by yet other factors which, if traced back long enough, lie outside the agent's control. But in either case, it would appear, the agent cannot act of his own free will, for if (1) the wants and beliefs arise spontaneously and randomly (which is what it is to say they have no causes), then the agent is at the helpless mercy of these eruptions within him which control his behavior, or if (2) the wants and beliefs are caused by other factors outside the agent's control, then the agent is at the helpless mercy of events over which he has no control. In either case, since he cannot act of his own free will, he should never be held morally responsible for what he does, and never deserves praise or blame, credit or discredit for his actions.

That no one should ever be held morally responsible for his actions is a most undesirable consequence. For our whole fabric of morality and our deep sense that men are morally responsible for what they do would have to be drastically modified if no one is ever responsible. There are those, to be sure, who accept this consequence and maintain that no one should be blamed or praised for what he does.[21] But most of us would wish to draw a line between those who should not be held responsible for their actions, the madmen, imbeciles, little children, sleepwalkers, the coerced and the duped, and those who should be held responsible, the sane, normal men who do things knowingly and without coercion. Surely if a man of the latter sort kills to gain wealth or lies to avoid disapproval, breaks a solemn promise for the sake of his own convenience or betrays a friend for the reward, most of us would believe he should be held morally responsible for his actions.

While most of us do believe men are sometimes morally responsible for what they do, we also believe that a man should be held responsible for what he did only if he could have done otherwise. If he could have done no other, if he could not help doing what he did, then he is not to be held responsible for doing it.

But if our decisions and actions have causes and if these causes either arise randomly or themselves have causes which eventually lie outside our control, then it would seem that we can do no other than what we did do and therefore are not responsible for our actions.

If we wish to continue to believe that sometimes men are responsible for their decisions and actions, what are the alternatives? We may deny that such decisions and actions ever have causes which lie outside the control of the agent (such a view is often called libertarianism), either because the notion of cause has no application to such decisions and actions (as performative theorists, goal theorists, and contextualists hold) or because the ultimate cause of such decisions and actions is simply the agent himself (as agency theorists hold). Or we may admit that such decisions and actions do have causes which ultimately lie outside the agent's control, but argue that a man nevertheless may be responsible for his decisions and actions.

Since we have noted certain advantages to the mental cause theory, let us see if a case can be made out on that theory for holding men responsible. Such a view does have an initial plausibility, for it would seem reasonable to say that a man was acting of his own free will if his decisions and actions were dictated by his own wants and beliefs, even if his wants and beliefs had causes which, if traced

[21] See John Hospers, "Free Will and Psychoanalysis," *Philosophy and Phenomenological Research*, 1950; it is reprinted in Paul Edwards and Arthur Pap, *A Modern Introduction to Philosophy*, rev. ed. (New York: The Free Press, 1965), pp. 75-85.

back far enough, lay beyond his control. If I do something just because I want to, or because I believe that doing it will get me what I want, just that sort of action would seem to be the paradigm of a voluntary action.

But now if we believe that our beliefs and wants cause our actions and that they have causes outside our control, then two facts seem to emerge showing that such acts are not acts of free will. (1) Since beliefs and wants cause our decisions and actions, it would seem that *we* do not seem to have control over our decisions and actions. Given our beliefs and wants, we *must* decide and act in a particular way and can do no other. And how could such decisions and actions be free? (2) Since the beliefs and wants themselves have causes beyond our control, we must want and believe what we do and therefore must decide and act as we do by virtue of factors beyond our control. And, again, how could such decisions and actions be free? How legitimate are these conclusions?

To (1), the mental cause theorist might reply that we must distinguish between causation and coercion. The fact that particular wants and beliefs *must* produce a particular decision in the sense that they *cause* it does not mean that the agent *must* make that decision in the sense that he was *forced* and *compelled* to make it *against his inclinations* or *despite his beliefs*. Quite the contrary, the agent's decision was formed precisely by those inclinations and beliefs. The causal efficacy of his wants and beliefs was not a constraint on his free will but the exercise of it. It is true that, with those beliefs and wants, *causally* he could do no other, but he could have done otherwise in the sense that with other wants or other beliefs he would have done otherwise. And it is the latter which is the relevant sense in which a man can be said to do something of his own free will.

Many contemporary philosophers do not find this reply satisfactory. They argue that for a man to be said to have acted of his own free will it is necessary that *in those circumstances* he could have done otherwise, and they reject an account of "could have done otherwise" as meaning that with other wants or other beliefs the man would have done otherwise. That a man would have done something else in other circumstances is quite irrelevant to whether he *could* have done something else in *these* circumstances. To say the decision was a free one is to say that, given those wants and beliefs the man had at the time, it was then and there in his power to do one thing or another. Consider the drug addict who wants a fix and believes that injecting himself with this needle will give him a fix, these reasons causing him to inject the needle. It is certainly true of this man that he would have acted differently if he had not had that want and that belief. But this does not mean that he injected the needle of his own free will. In fact, as we well know, he could not help himself; his act was not voluntary. And now, what difference is there between the drug addict, whose actions are caused by his wants and beliefs, and the rest of us? The reply of the libertarian is that for the rest of us, at least, when we act freely, our actions are *not caused* by our wants and beliefs.

The mental cause theorist does owe us some account of the difference between the drug addict's "compulsive" taking of the drug and our ordinary, free actions. The following suggestion might have some merit. What distinguishes the drug addict's case is that his desire is "irresistible," and an "irresistible" desire is a desire that would lead someone to act *no matter what he believed the further consequences of the action would be*. Thus, the addict would inject the needle even if he believed it would result in the ruination of his family and himself, even their deaths, even his own death. Now we often know of our actions that if we had believed that the action would have had particular undesirable consequences, then we would not have acted that way. Perhaps that is the sort of thing we mean when we say we did not have to act that way and could have acted otherwise, whereas the drug addict had to act that way and could not have acted otherwise. If that is the sort of thing we mean, then the difference between the drug addict's actions and our normal ones is not that his had a cause whereas ours do not. It is that the cause of his action was so powerful that no further considerations could have prevented it from causing the action, whereas the cause of a normal action would not lead to that action if certain further considerations were taken into account. How satisfactory a reply this is must be left to the reader to decide; the matter is still very controversial at this time.

To (2), the objection that if we cannot help having the beliefs and wants we do have, then we cannot help doing the actions they cause us to do, the mental cause theorist might reply that the conclusion does not follow. The argument is based upon the assumption that if something, A, has a property (in this case, of being something we cannot help), and if A causes B, then B must have that property also. Although this assumption may hold for some properties, it obviously does not hold for all; medicine which we do not like may cause better health which we do like. It is true that if A causes B and B causes C, A can be said to cause C, so that it can be said, on the mental cause thesis, that what causes our wants and beliefs can be said to cause our actions. But it does not follow from this that what causes our wants and beliefs *despite our will* necessarily causes our actions *despite our will*. And, in the case where wants and beliefs *affect our will*, it is obviously false that what causes our wants and beliefs despite our will causes our actions despite our will. For the mental cause theorist, events beyond our control which cause our wants and beliefs result in actions which are under our control. But the mental cause theorist still owes us an analysis of what it is for something to be *under our control*. And perhaps a suggested analysis on the lines of the paragraph above will prove satisfactory.

In this chapter, we have examined in some detail the concept of intentional actions, one of the concepts central to the notion of consciousness. Insofar as it has been shown to involve the concepts of belief, desire, and decision, the concept of intentional actions exemplifies all three aspects of the hallowed triad of cognition, affection, and volition. We could further pursue the study of the philosophy of mind by asking ourselves what it is to *believe* something or *desire* something or *choose* something. Or we could now move off in other directions, turning to other central concepts like perception, memory, imagination, attention, etc. But perhaps enough has been done here to give the reader some idea of the complexity, importance, and interest of the philosophy of mind.

For further reading

The book which most stimulated contemporary interest in the philosophy of mind was Gilbert Ryle's *The Concept of Mind*, first published in 1949. It still overshadows any other single work in the field. It is listed below with other important recent works by individual authors. The anthologies which follow contain important recent journal articles, although some, such as those of Flew and Vesey, contain pertinent extracts from the great philosophers of the past as well. Bibliographies of further readings can be found in many of the anthologies. I have also included a list of relevant articles from Paul Edwards' *The Encyclopedia of Philosophy*. These articles, written by leading experts, are of very high quality and include useful bibliographies on the particular topics.

Works by Individual Authors

Anscombe, G. E. M., *Intention*. Ithaca, N.Y.: Cornell University Press, 1958. Paperback.

Armstrong, David M., *Bodily Sensations*. New York: Humanities Press (London: Routledge & Kegan Paul, Ltd.), 1962.

Feigl, Herbert, *The "Mental" and the "Physical."* Minneapolis: University of Minnesota Press, 1967. Paperback.

Hampshire, Stuart, *The Freedom of the Individual*. New York: Harper and Row, Publishers, 1965.

————, *Thought and Action*. New York: Viking Press, 1960.

Kenny, Anthony, *Action, Emotion, and Will*. New York: Humanities Press (London: Routledge & Kegan Paul, Ltd.), 1963.

MacIntyre, Alasdair C., *The Unconscious: A Conceptual Analysis*. New York: Humanities Press (London: Routledge & Kegan Paul, Ltd.), 1958.

Melden, A. I., *Free Action*. New York: Humanities Press (London: Routledge & Kegan Paul, Ltd.), 1961.

Peters, R. S., *The Concept of Motivation* (2nd ed.). New York: Humanities Press (London: Routledge & Kegan Paul, Ltd.), 1960.
Ryle, Gilbert, *The Concept of Mind*. New York: Barnes & Noble, Inc., 1949. Also in paperback: Baltimore: Penguin Books.
Shoemaker, Sydney, *Self-Knowledge and Self-Identity*. Ithaca, N.Y.: Cornell University Press, 1963.
Shwayder, David S., *The Stratification of Behavior*. New York: Humanities Press (London: Routledge & Kegan Paul, Ltd.), 1965.
Smythies, J. R., *The Neurological Foundations of Psychiatry*. New York: Academic Press (Oxford: Blackwell Scientific Publications), 1966.
Taylor, Charles, *The Explanation of Behavior*. New York: Humanities Press (London: Routledge & Kegan Paul, Ltd.), 1964.
Taylor, Richard, *Action and Purpose*. Englewood Cliffs, N.J.: Prentice-Hall, Inc., 1966.
Vesey, G. N. A., *The Embodied Mind*. New York: Humanities Press (London: George Allen and Unwin, Ltd.), 1965.
White, Alan R., *Attention*. Oxford: Basil Blackwell & Mott, Ltd., 1965.
———, *Explaining Human Behavior*. Hull University Press, 1962.
———, *The Philosophy of Mind*. New York: Random House, 1967. Paperback.
Wisdom, John O., *Other Minds*. Oxford: Basil Blackwell & Mott, Ltd., 1965.
Wittgenstein, Ludwig, *Philosophical Investigations*, trans. G. E. M. Anscombe (2nd ed.). New York: The Macmillan Company (Oxford: Basil Blackwell & Mott, Ltd.), 1958.

Anthologies

Anderson, Alan R., ed., *Minds and Machines*. Englewood Cliffs, N.J.: Prentice-Hall, Inc., 1964. Paperback.
Berofsky, Bernard, ed., *Free Will and Determinism*. New York: Harper and Row, Publishers, 1966.
Chappell, Vere C., ed., *The Philosophy of Mind*. Englewood Cliffs, N.J.: Prentice-Hall, Inc., 1962. A Spectrum book.
Flew, Antony, ed., *Body, Mind, and Death*. New York: The Macmillan Company, 1964. Paperback.
Gustafson, Donald F., ed., *Essays in Philosophical Psychology*. Garden City, N.Y.: Doubleday & Company, Inc., 1964. An Anchor book.
Hampshire, Stuart, ed., *Philosophy of Mind*. New York: Harper and Row, Publishers, 1966. Paperback.
Hook, Sidney, ed., *Determinism and Freedom: In the Age of Modern Science*. New York: Collier Books, 1961. Paperback.
———, *Dimensions of Mind: A Symposium*. New York: New York University Press, 1960.
Lehrer, Keith, ed., *Freedom and Determinism*. New York: Random House, 1966.
Pears, D. F., ed., *Freedom and the Will*. New York: St. Martins Press (London: Macmillan and Company, Ltd.), 1963.
Smythies, J. R., ed., *Mind and Brain*. New York: Humanities Press (London: Routledge & Kegan Paul, Ltd.), 1965.

Vesey, G. N. A., ed., *Body and Mind*. New York: Humanities Press (London: George Allen and Unwin, Ltd.), 1964.

Wann, T. W., ed., *Behaviorism and Phenomenology*. Chicago: The University of Chicago Press, 1966. A Phoenix book.

Encyclopedia articles

The following are relevant articles in Paul Edwards, ed., *The Encyclopedia of Philosophy* (New York: The Macmillan Company, 1967):

Behaviorism
Can
Choosing, Deciding
and Doing
Consciousness
Death
Determinism
Dreams
Emotion and Feeling
ESP Phenomena
Experience
Freedom
Happiness

Ideas
Images
Imagination
Immortality
Intention
Intentionality
Materialism
Memory
Mind-Body Problem
Motives and
Motivation
Other Minds
Perception

Personal Identity
Persons
Phenomenology
Philosophical
Anthropology
Pleasure
Private Language
Problem
Reasons and Causes
Responsibility
Thinking
Unconsciousness
Volition
Voluntarism

INDEX